What Other *Everyday* Pec

"This book isn't like the others I've read as the stories are real life and most importantly attainable. Once I started, I had a hard time putting it down. I've already passed this book along to friends with many others asking about it."
- Jason Tansem; Publisher

"This was one of the best books I've ever read because they were real life cases. I learned the most so far from EVERYDAY *Real Estate* MILLIONAIRES™ & the Rich Dad® series." **- Jim Koumanis; MD**

"Wealthy Barber for Real Estate Investor! I could not put it down and plan to read it a 2nd & 3rd time. My wife never reads financial books, yet she picked up EVERYDAY *Real Estate* MILLIONAIRES™ every time I put it down." **- Jeffrey Burgis, Sales, BC**

"Simply Sensational! I've read a lot of real estate books but NOW I have finally found the roadmap and the mentor! This book delivers creative, calculated ideas and actions with measureable, step by step results!"
- Dawn King, Author of Living a Vibrant Life

"Invaluable resource for anyone who desires to be a Real Estate Investor but never knew where to start. Provides an eye-opener to the truth." **- Carol Kirkland, Retiree**

"There have been countless books, seminars and even reality TV shows around real estate investing. Much of it is based on HYPE and GET RICH QUICK schemes. This book DOES NOT belong in that category! You'll see the choices made in order to move forward during difficult times. Once I started, I had a hard time putting the book down." - **Darryl Kelly, Real Estate Investor, AB**

Reading EVERYDAY Real Estate MILLIONAIRES™ made me feel like I was on the same level as the investors in the book, as opposed to being preached at by so-called "gurus." The stories felt like they could have come from my neighbor as I read about their real struggles with life's every day challenges. An easy read with simple to grasp concepts!" - **Leigh Dawson, BCOM, Investor**

"EVERYDAY Real Estate MILLIONAIRES™ was hard to put down! It was so interesting that I passed it on to my wife." - **Rob Tilman, Author of Xtrapreneur**

"Not your typical real estate investing book - perfect for the novice right up to the advanced investor. The tips and ways around traditional financing really opened my eyes. I have read most investing books out there, and they all repeat the same vague message, never giving out the real "tricks" of the trade. This book actually does!
- **Traci Thompson, RE/MAX REALTOR® & Investor**

www.PAULMHECHT.com

"Paul Hecht inspires investors to become more. I love the real life applications and scenarios in EVERYDAY Real Estate MILLIONAIRES™. It is a must have book to keep with you always. Seeing Paul speak live is even more captivating than his book." - **Rod O'Keefe, OMREIC Investor Club, BC**

"Paul's book simply opened my eyes to what creative things can be done. I enjoyed the real life stories or REAL everyday people who took big steps, small steps, failed, succeeded and overcame obstacles. Paul has a great story and trust me when I say - he will motivate you!" - **Janey Kasprzak, Sparkling Hill Wellness Resort**

"Hey Paul, I just want to thank you for wonderful advice, your honesty, the depth of your email Newsletter and what you wrote in your book EVERYDAY Real Estate MILLIONAIRES™" - **Chris Doell, Contractor**

"There are so many books and gurus around telling you to buy real estate with no money down, but none of them have any really practical (or legal) advice on how to do it. The strategies in this book are as simple as investing gets and don't operate in the gray-areas of the law. Best of all, anybody can invest this way - age, credit rating, bank account balance... none of it matters. You can be bankrupt and broke and still make it with these ideas" - **Phillip Theriault; CEO Spellweaver Technologies**

"I gotta tell you, EVERYDAY Real Estate MILLIONAIRES™ is fantastic! I was excited about RE before I started reading this, but now I am more confident that I can really do this. What a practical book. One of the easiest books to read that I've ever picked up - it's just everyday people talking straight to me. Great amount of info and tips from a practical point of view - Thanks Paul." - **Linda Sue Norvell, Woodland Hills, CA**

"I've read all the other books and taken many seminars. Nothing beats real life experience and Paul definitely has that." - **Warren Hansen, RE/MAX REALTOR®**

"I truly recommend Paul Hecht's training, his book EVERYDAY Real Estate MILLIONAIRES and him as a person to help you along in your journey to be a real estate investor and millionaire. He is down to earth, very accessible and everyday people can relate to him." - **Alicia Dunams, Author of GoalDigger**

"I have already given away 3 copies of this book to friends because this book is about real lives and real people!" - **Rofida Kaboli, Tenant**

"I couldn't sleep after I finished this book! My daughter is equally excited to know that she doesn't have to be an employee for 30+ years before she is able to do what she truly wants." - **Hazel Dawson, Investor**

www.PAULMHECHT.com

EVERYDAY
Real Estate
MILLIONAIRES™

~ v ~

www.PAULMHECHT.com

EVERYDAY
Real Estate
MILLIONAIRES™

HOW AVERAGE PEOPLE *REALLY* DO IT

PAUL M. HECHT

www.PAULMHECHT.com

EVERYDAY REAL ESTATE MILLIONAIRES™
How Average People REALLY Do It!
© Copyright 2008, 2009 by Paul M. Hecht. All rights reserved.
SECOND EDITION

EVERYDAY REAL ESTATE MILLIONAIRES™ is the property of Inspired Wealth Corp.

Cover by: George Foster of Foster Covers

Distributed in Canada and the United States of America
Printed in the United States of America

This book is printed on recycled paper at the author's request.
ISBN-10: 0-9769300-6-4
ISBN-13: 978-0-9769300-6-8

www.PAULMHECHT.com

This book is dedicated to my mother
~ Lesley Margaret Hecht --
1943 – 1988

www.PAULMHECHT.com

Everyday Real Estate Millionaires™

~ x ~

www.PAULMHECHT.com

ACKNOWLEDGEMENTS

First and foremost, I would like to thank the people who shared their true life stories in this book. Had you not had the courage to challenge yourselves and break down the many barriers and obstacles you faced on your paths, this book would not have been possible.

To my wife for your continuous belief in me, your constant support and the long hours you put in making this book what it is today, I cannot thank you enough.

To my father for your unwavering example of patience, humility and unconditional love, to my mother for your kindness and tenderness, and to my big brother for the countless hours of philosophical debates about anything and everything; many thanks.

To Kjarlune Rae, I thank you for your guidance, insight and love.

To the editors, graphic artists, publisher, fulfillment company and distributors of this book, I thank you for making this book a physical reality.

www.PAULMHECHT.com

Last but not least, a sincere thank you to all the readers of this book for letting me share these inspirational stories with you.

CONTENTS

www.PAULMHECHT.com

www.PAULMHECHT.com

ABOUT THE AUTHOR

Paul M. Hecht, bought and sold his first property at the age of twenty one using none of his own money or credit. Ninety days later, he had resold the property and made over $5,000.00. He has been investing in real estate in one form or another ever since.

Paul's extensive real estate knowledge came through both education and real life experience. Never one to believe everything he read or was told, he found that the best way to learn was by doing.

Paul's vast and varied investment experience includes property flips, rentals, rehabs, lease options and rent-to-owns, pre-foreclosures and selling contracts. From single family to multi-family apartment buildings and condominium conversions, he has acquired property as a principal as well as numerous joint ventures.

As Paul's expertise increased, he decided to share what he had learned with others. He began speaking at various events internationally, training both groups and individuals on the ins and outs of investing in real estate. From beginners to the most advanced investors, some with little money to spare, others with thousands

~ 15 ~

or even millions to invest, many have benefited from Paul's insight, know-how and investment acumen.

In the meantime, while pursuing his dream of financial freedom, Paul made the grave mistake of investing all his resources into one single business and put all his trust into his new partners. When the business failed, Paul struggled to repay the debt personally. After a year of trying to make ends meet, he was forced to declare bankruptcy.

With a wife and two small children at home, with no money and no credit, he did not have the luxury of wallowing or regrouping. He turned to what he knew and loved the most – real estate. With hard work and perseverance, in just twenty four months he became a Self-Made Real Estate Millionaire.

These days, Paul continues to invest in real estate. He maintains ownership in a wide variety of income properties and continues to build his real estate investment portfolio.

As an investor, author, public speaker, trainer and real estate agent, Paul continues to share his wealth of knowledge with others. He encourages and inspires individuals and audiences alike by proving that an average person starting out against the odds, can

www.PAULMHECHT.com

become financially free and live the life they've always dreamed of.

Whether your real estate market is booming or busting is irrelevant. Paul's proven real estate investment strategies show real people how to make real money in any type of market.

www.PAULMHECHT.com

INTRODUCTION

At the age of 33, I was bankrupt. Twenty four months later, I became a self made real estate millionaire. Since then, I have had many people ask me how I did it. That got me thinking.

While there are hundreds of theoretically based real estate reference books published, very few demonstrate how regular people actually make money with real estate. What were the steps that they took? How did they really get from point A to point B, then C and so on? Even fewer books show the pitfalls or struggles that people encountered along the way.

It also dawned on me that many people, like myself, tend to learn more and retain more from real life experience - whether it's their own or someone else's – than they do from technical reference material. While people obviously need the basic tools to get started, many aren't sure how to proceed once their education is in place.

Being involved in real estate for a great part of my life, I have had the privilege of meeting numerous real estate investors – some dabble, some invest full time, and others fall somewhere in between. Every one of the people I have met has had their own reason for investing in real estate. While some investors share similar experiences, every path has been unique and every outcome has been somewhat different.

EVERYDAY REAL ESTATE MILLIONAIRES™ came about because I wanted to share my experiences, my path and the ups and downs that I encountered along the way. I also included the stories of three other real estate investors to demonstrate that there are many ways to make money in real estate. There are many roads to take, and while these roads might have some unexpected twists and turns, they are also paved with unexpected benefits and rewards.

I wrote this book to demonstrate that regular, everyday people CAN make money with real estate. Not only can they make money, but if they choose to, they can make a great deal of money and have the financial freedom to be able to live their lives however they wish.

Not only is EVERYDAY REAL ESTATE MILLIONAIRES™ meant to inform and educate through the use of real life examples, it is meant to inspire, motivate and encourage others to take steps in their own lives to gain control and live the life of their dreams.

I hope that you enjoy the stories included in this book. For those of you who want to invest in real estate but are afraid to get started, I hope that these stories give you the confidence to take the first step towards your first investment. For those of you who already invest in real estate, I hope that these stories either help you discover something new about real estate investment or reinforce that you are on the right path. For those of you who have already achieved real estate success, I commend you on your accomplishments and can appreciate the many challenges that you have already overcome.

Regardless of where you are today or where you may be headed, I hope that these stories prompt you to take at least one step forward towards turning your goals, ambitions and dreams into reality.

Enjoy!

Sincerely,

Paul M. Hecht

Author | Speaker | Investment Coach | Real Estate Agent

STORY ONE

CAM

IT'S HOW & WHY YOU PLAY THE GAME

"The ultimate measure of a man is not where he stands in moments of comfort, but where he stands at times of challenge and controversy."

~ Martin Luther King, Jr.

I did not come from a wealthy family, nor was I given any hand outs when I left home at eighteen. I've had to earn every dime I've ever made.

The small farming community where I lived had a population of approximately 14,000 people. My two brothers, two sisters and I were raised in a traditional family setting. My dad worked his 9-5 job and my mom raised us and took care of the household.

My father was an insurance agent and after working for the same company for almost twenty loyal years, he was given the pink slip. As he was laid off three years before his retirement, he did not receive the full company pension that he was counting on.

Without any investments, very little savings and a diminished pension, he did not have enough to retire. Selling our home was not an option since the equity was not enough to retire on either. Therefore he still needed to work.

He decided to go into business for himself and opened a small insurance agency. While he did have almost twenty years experience in the field, being a sales agent and running a profitable insurance business required completely different skills. Without any significant money in the bank, my father took a large risk going out on his own.

After struggling for several years in business, with debt piled up too high for him to bear, my father declared bankruptcy. His business had failed.

My mother was completely devastated. The long hours, meager profits, sacrifices and stress that went along with the new business had all been for nothing. My mother could no longer take it. My parents divorced, sold our family home and each moved into separate rental properties. My dad was humiliated and felt like life had let him down. He never really got over it.

Almost nine years later, my father passed away from cancer. He died empty and unfulfilled. The pain and struggle that my parents underwent prior to my father's death and the grief that my mother endured made an impression on my young mind.

Those last few years of my life at home shaped my future. I vowed that when I had my own family, I would never put them in that position. I would provide my family with financial stability and security, so that no matter what happened, their lives would not be uprooted. I decided that I would do whatever it took to make that happen. I wasn't exactly sure how that was going to happen, but I was committed to finding a way.

When I did finally leave home, I struggled to make ends meet. Regardless, I put my self through university by doing two things.

I worked part-time in the evenings and on weekends and full-time every summer. The second thing I did was instead of using all of my student loans for school and living expenses, I invested the majority of them into mutual funds. At the time, mutual funds were quite new and performed very well – much better than they do today.

When my schooling was complete, I used my mutual fund profits to pay off my student loans. I had the huge advantage of not having those loans hang over me for years.

I worked hard, completed my education and graduated with honors. With my business degree and CGA designation in hand, I had the world at my fingertips. Or, so I thought.

I was immediately offered several positions with different companies. I took one that had a decent starting salary and good reputation. It was a place where

I could advance and had benefits. However, it did not take me long to figure out that a steady job alone would not provide me with the financial stability that I craved.

As I made and counted other people's money, I had the desire to spend more time educating myself on how to create my own wealth. I read many books and learned everything I could about money and wealth so that when I had my own family, I would not have to face the financial hardship I saw in my parents' lives.

Because of frequent market shifts and the volatility of the stock market, I decided that real estate was the safest way to do it. Real estate was tangible and if the market ever crashed, at least I would have a real building that could still generate income or at the very least be sold for land value and materials. If I invested in stocks and the stock market crashed, all I had were worthless pieces of paper.

So, I decided I would pursue real estate. I made that decision nine years ago and as a result, my life is very different. Today, if I sold everything that I control, I could live for the next fifty one years with my current lifestyle, without working another day.

I am currently married with one child at home and another on the way. I am thrilled to know that I have been able to provide my family with the security that my parents never realized. While I am unable to predict the future, at least I've prepared for it to the best of my ability.

These days, I invest in real estate more for the challenge than the paycheck. Acquiring the first million in wealth took almost eight years. The second million was acquired within one year after that. It's hard to imagine that the second million took only 1/8th the time to obtain. However, that's how it worked. Once I had the knowledge and momentum going, along with the discipline to stick to my plan, the money started to compound quickly.

It was very tempting to become complacent or drunk with the money and spend it on fancy cars and an extravagant lifestyle. However, discipline was the way I acquired my wealth in the first place and that did not change. The way I live is probably not how you would think a multi-millionaire would live.

I drive a six year old pickup truck and I recently purchased a second vehicle for my wife to use. This recent acquisition was a second hand three year old SUV that we found with low mileage at a great price. We buy second hand vehicles since the largest depreciation happens within the first 1-3 years.

I do not look primarily at the purchase price or monthly payments when I buy a vehicle. I look more at the percentage of my net worth compared to the vehicle's value. My total vehicle's value never exceeds 1% of my total net worth. When my net worth was lower, this percentage was higher.

We live in a well located neighborhood of single-family homes with a very low crime rate and excellent schools. The average price of homes in our city is currently $378,000.00. Our current home is now worth $445,000.00. I bought it eight years ago with a low down payment. That was my third property.

INVESTMENT TIP:

IT IS WISE TO BUY ONE OF THE LOWEST PRICED PROPERTIES IN A GOOD NEIGHBOURHOOD

The value of our home has increased more than 10% per year. We only put down $13,000.00 and now have over $300,000.00 in equity.

With our current wealth, we could very easily purchase a million-dollar home. However, we have just upgraded to a three-bedroom bungalow in the same neighborhood for $465,000.00 and we just sold our two bedroom home for $445,000.00.

Over the years, my goal has been to reinvest my profits and not spend them on frivolous items. By doing this I was able to put as much money back into real estate as I could in order to grow at a quicker pace. While there are times that I have to use some profits for our living expenses, we keep our living expenses as low as possible so that we can continue to invest.

One thing that keeps our living expenses so low is that other than a mortgage on our home and the mortgages on our investment properties, we have zero personal debt. Even when I started out on my own, I always kept my personal debt very low. The memory of my childhood has never been far from my mind.

I purchase all my investment properties through a corporation of which my wife and I are shareholders. Therefore all the income, expenses and mortgage debt is run through a separate entity and not me personally.

My real estate investments are my business. By running my real estate business through corporate entities, I get legal protection as well as effective tax planning. This way I am allowed to take money out of the company at very reasonable tax rates and continue to accumulate wealth.

My company also pays for our business vehicles, gas, insurance and many other expenses that are not available to regular employees. When I was an employee, I didn't appreciate the fact that employees paid the most in taxes and that those taxes were their largest lifetime expense.

For me it's not about how much you make, it's about how much you keep. I have never drawn a salary from my own company - a principle I continue to maintain to this day.

I started using a corporate entity after I purchased my second property. I knew that I would be purchasing more real estate and wanted to pay the least amount of tax that I legally could. Since real estate investment was my business, it made sense for me to run the income and profits through a corporation.

You might be wondering how I went from being an accounting controller with an interest in real estate investment to a full-time investor with a net worth into the millions. To be honest with you, it was a combination of self-education, hard work, discipline, determination and patience.

When I first made the decision to start investing in real estate, I made a commitment to myself to give it my best shot.

INVESTMENT TIP:

IF YOUR ONLY INCOME IS FROM AN HOURLY RATE, THEN YOUR WEALTH IS LIMITED BY THE NUMBER OF HOURS YOU WORK.

As I had made a decent wage as a controller and my living expenses were low, I had the ability to save a fair bit of money. I used this money for a down payment on my first house.

While looking for my first property, I realized that the real estate market was almost flat. This meant that real estate values were increasing at about 1% - 3% per year for several years in a row. The economy was slowly picking up as I entered the market and real estate values started to increase approximately 4% - 6% per year.

While searching for my first property, I kept in mind that I wanted something that was not going to be a financial strain on me personally.

I found and purchased a two bedroom bungalow in a good neighborhood, with a rental suite in the basement. The house was on a busier street which made the price lower. Actually, it was one of the lowest priced properties in the neighborhood. Even though it was on a busy street, the rent I could collect was not proportionately lower than one on a quieter street in the same neighborhood.

I lived on the main floor, rented out the two other bedrooms and also rented out the one bedroom basement suite. The rent I collected from the basement suite plus my roommates' rent covered my mortgage, taxes, insurance, utilities and maintenance for the property. Therefore my cost of living was even less than when I was paying rent on my own. All I had to buy was my food, clothing and anything else that I required.

With my cost of living even lower than before, I used my salary to make extra mortgage payments each month in addition to saving for my next property. I also made lump sum payments onto the mortgage once a year. By doing this, I paid off the first mortgage in five years.

Needless to say I made many sacrifices in my lifestyle during that time. My success would not have been possible if I had lived like my colleagues who bought fancy clothes, nice cars, ate at nice restaurants and went on lavish holidays. I was disciplined and focused on building my wealth and did what ever it took, legally.

For example, one New Year's day I received a phone call from an old college buddy. He was lying on a beach in Mexico and I was adding up the number of drywall sheets I needed for one of my renovation projects. Need I say more?

Three years after I had purchased the first property, I had paid off a large portion of the mortgage and was eager to purchase a second property.

I went to the bank to apply for mortgage number two to purchase a second property. While I still had a full time job, my banker said that I could not qualify for another mortgage because I already had a mortgage as well as a truck payment. It came down to the fact that my vehicle payment was standing between me and my second property.

I'd be lying if I didn't say that I was disappointed. You see, I had just purchased that new truck. It was my gift to myself for staying so disciplined.

However the decision was very easy as I understood that real estate would buy many vehicles at a future date. I ended up selling my truck so that I did not have a vehicle loan payment and could therefore qualify for the second mortgage. I signed the mortgage papers the following week.

Most people, including my banker, could not believe that I sold the truck and took the bus to work in order to buy another property. For me the decision was easy. That temporary inconvenience was for a greater future reward.

INVESTMENT TIP:

PERSONAL MONTHLY DEBT PAYMENTS FOR CAR LOANS AND CREDIT CARDS DEMINISH YOUR ABILITY TO QUAILIFY FOR A LOAN OR MORTGAGE.

Property number two was similar to the first one. It was another house with a suite in the basement. Once again, I purchased one of the lowest priced properties in a good neighborhood. I decided to rent it out.

The second property's rental income covered all its operating costs including mortgage, property taxes, insurance, maintenance allowance and a small management fee that I had built in for myself. If I wanted to hire a property management company, there was enough income to pay someone else to manage the property. I ended up self managing the property for the entire time I owned it. It was a lot easier than I thought it would be.

The third house I bought was the one we were currently living in and just sold. Again, it was one of the lowest priced homes in the neighborhood. It had two bedrooms on the main floor and an unfinished basement.

When we initially purchased it, it had been on the market for a few months with no offers. It was on a good street with a good sized lot and had the potential to be fixed up. My plan was to move in and fix it up slowly with any extra money I made from work.

Since it was my principal residence, I only had to put down 5%. Once again I used the money I had saved from my salary. Saving money from my job had worked well for me and it was the way I got started. However, I realized that it was taking a long time to save enough money for each property.

The more I made at my job, the more I paid in taxes. I needed a way to make more money so that I could invest more. Actually, it dawned on me that I really didn't need a way to make more; I just needed a way to keep more. I started to pay close attention to what my accountant's clients were doing with their businesses.

I noticed that all the clients who were self employed or had their own business paid a smaller percentage of income tax than an employee. They had more options available to them to pay less in tax, which in turn, put more money in their pockets. I paid attention.

If I had my own business, I would pay far less in taxes which meant that I would keep more money in my own pocket. I knew just the perfect business: real estate.

After working as a controller for over six years and acquiring three properties, I was tired of working for 5% raises and dealing with office politics. I was ready to make my move. It was time to leave my job and put what I had learned into practice. I quit my well paying job and exchanged my employee income for self employed income.

Given that my living expenses where next to nothing (my tenants were paying my mortgage, property tax and insurance), I did not need a great deal of money to survive. That said, since I no longer had a steady paycheck, I would still need to generate some money to pay the bills and feed myself.

I decided to cash in my retirement savings plan. I then put the money in the bank to cover my living expenses while I pursued my real estate business. Because I was technically unemployed when I cashed in my retirement plan, I paid very little in income tax and penalties.

INVESTMENT TIP:

CASHING INVESTMENTS DURING PERIODS WHEN YOUR PERSONAL INCOME IS LOW REDUCES THE AMOUNT OF INCOME TAX YOU MAY HAVE TO PAY.

I also chose to refinance my first property. Since I had been making extra mortgage payments on that property, the mortgage had already been paid off. (It had only taken five years.) By doing this, I could use the cash to invest in more real estate.

My next step was to build as much capital as possible. I wanted to grow my business quickly and the more money I had, the more real estate I could buy. I needed something that could generate large amounts of cash. I concluded that my best bet would be to buy rundown properties, renovate them and sell them for a profit.

~ 38 ~

As my skills as a handyman had increased over the years, I realized that I could save money by completing most of the renovation work myself. Any skills that I did not possess could easily be hired out.

With my decision made, I went straight to work to find the right property. Once again I focused on lower priced properties in the better neighborhoods that required only cosmetic improvements.

INVESTMENT TIP:

WHEN SEARCHING FOR THE RIGHT INVESTMENT, PATIENCE IS CRITICAL. THERE IS ALWAYS ANOTHER DEAL.

I looked at approximately eighty homes before I found it. It was a three bedroom bungalow and I paid $180,000.00. Looking at those eighty homes helped me to understand the market and it also gave me the confidence to recognize a good deal.

The money that I obtained from the refinancing of my first property was used for the down payment and the renovations. Since I was self employed, I had to put down more money than I had in the past.

The whole project lasted approximately six months. This included the time that I waited to take ownership of the property, renovated it, listed it for sale, found the buyer and waited for the sale to close.

All in all, I invested $47,000.00. This amount included the down payment, renovation costs and holding costs. After real estate commissions and legal fees, I realized a profit of $23,000.00. I turned my $47,000.00 into $70,000.00 in six months - a 47% return on my money.

With that property out of the way, I was on the hunt for the next flip. My real estate agent found the second one about two weeks after we started searching. Once again, it was one of the lower priced homes in a good neighborhood and required only cosmetic improvements. It was listed for $235,000.00. I paid $227,000.00.

This time, between the down payment, renovation costs and holding costs I had invested $59,000.00. After real estate commissions and legal fees, I walked away with a $30,000.00 profit. I had turned my $70,000.00 into $100,000.00.

By completing two renovation projects in one year, I turned my $47,000.00 initial investment into $100,000.00. I had more than doubled my money.

I hadn't made the same amount of money with real estate that I had made with my previous job. However, the biggest difference was that being self employed allowed me more tax deductions and therefore I kept more of the money that I did make.

I also found that with each project I learned ways to save money and make the renovation more appealing to buyers. Therefore my profits had the potential to increase. If I could continue to double my money every year, I would soon far exceed my annual salary.

In the past I was led to believe that the higher the rate of return in an investment, the greater the risk. I made over a 100% return on my money by flipping two houses in one year. My money was secured by real estate and if I could not sell it, I could always rent it out to cover my monthly costs.

I decided that just for fun, I would run some numbers to see where I would be in five years if I could continue to double my money.

I saw that I could grow my money at a much faster rate than my previous salary. Here's the chart that I calculated.

R.O.I. CHART	25 % ROI	50% ROI	100% ROI
Initial Capital	**$50,000.00**	**$50,000.00**	**$50,000.00**
12 months (1 yr)	$62,500.00	$75,000.00	$100,000.00
24 months (2 yrs)	$78,125.00	$112,500.00	$200,000.00
36 months (3 yrs)	$97,656.25	$168,750.00	$400,000.00
48 months (4 yrs)	$122,070.31	$253,125.00	$800,000.00
60 months (5 yrs)	**$152,587.88**	**$379,687.50**	**$1,600,000.00**
72 months (6 yrs)	$190,734.85	$569,531.25	
84 months (7 yrs)	$238,418.56	$854,296.87	
96 months (8 yrs)	**$298,023.20**	**$1,281,445.30**	
108 months (9 yrs)	$372,529.00		
120 months (10 yrs)	$465,661.25		
132 months (11 yrs)	$582,076.56		
144 months (12 yrs)	$727,595.70		
156 months (13 yrs)	$909,494.62		
168 months (14 yrs)	**$1,136,868.20**		

After examining that chart and realizing what I had accomplished, I still took a conservative approach and focused on increasing my net worth by 30% per year. (While that has remained my goal over the years, in reality, not only have I accomplished that target, but I have achieved over a 100% increase in my net worth year after year.)

After the two renovation flips, I took the profits and bought a side-by-side duplex to add another rental property to my portfolio. The property was run down so

I put my renovation skills to work and completed a minor renovation on the property. This property had two rental units – one on each side. I built an additional rental suite in the basement on one side so that I had three units from which to collect rent.

After the renovation, I rented the property to tenants who again covered the mortgage, tax, insurance and expenses. By renovating it, I was able to ask for higher rents from tenants who could afford more. Plus, my ongoing maintenance was next to nothing since everything had been fixed during the renovation. Therefore my monthly costs were reduced and again I could keep more of the money that I made.

There were two other factors that helped out with the purchase of the duplex. One was that I had bought the property on New Years Eve when no one else was buying. That paid off when lender's appraisal showed the market value as $30,000.00 higher than what I paid for it.

The second was that I was able to obtain the property with a low down payment. I had asked the seller to carry part of the down payment as seller financing. I made monthly payments to him instead of coming up with the entire down payment in cash. The seller became the bank. He did not need all the cash and was willing to receive a monthly payment instead.

Since I did not have to put down as much money for the down payment, this enabled me to use my own cash to renovate the property, thus increasing the value immediately.

INVESTMENT TIP:

SELLER FINANCING ALLOWS YOU TO BUY MORE PROPERTIES WITH LESS MONEY.

It took about ninety days to build the third suite in the basement and complete the minor renovations.

Since my goal was to increase the value with a renovation, I ordered an appraisal upon its completion. The value had increased, but not quite enough to make it worthwhile to refinance. I held the property for six more months and at that point the value had increased enough to warrant the refinancing.

With four properties in my possession, and six years of real estate investment experience, I was ready to tackle something bigger – an apartment building.

My goal was to find a run down apartment building, fix it up and increase the rents. The higher rents would increase the value enough to refinance the property and pull out all of the invested money. The building could then be held as a long term rental property. Before that could happen, I had to generate enough cash to purchase the building.

INVESTMENT TIP:

YOU CAN USE THE EQUITY IN YOUR OWN HOME OR OTHER PROPERTIES THAT YOU OWN, TO PURCHASE MORE REAL ESTATE.

I decided to sell the first two rental properties that I had purchased. The combination of increasing real estate values and several years of paying down the mortgage had netted me a nice profit. I set some of those profits aside to go towards the apartment building purchase.

I then refinanced my personal residence. That money, along with the money I had received from refinancing the duplex, was also put towards my goal.

With some money set aside, I was ready for my next task – finding a partner.

Purchasing an apartment building came with its own set of challenges – financing, scope of the work and scale to name a few. I knew that I wanted a partner to share in both the efforts, risks and the rewards.

I wanted a partner with integrity, strong morals and good work ethic. I wanted someone who had the desire to take on a larger project and possessed the skills that I did not have. They also had to have real estate investment experience and the capital to match mine. It took about six months to find a partner but after much searching I found him through my financial planner.

My soon-to-be partner was in the business of buying rundown single-family properties in good locations, mainly for land value. He would tear down the old house and build two new single-family houses on the same piece of land. He had been doing this for several years and was also interested in scaling up his business.

His formal training and experience was in architecture which gave him creative skills and renovation vision as well as permit and building code knowledge. I had cost control and business experience along with the contacts to help us complete a larger project.

We got straight to work in locating the right apartment building for our plan. After looking for about eight months, we located and purchased an eleven unit apartment building.

While we were looking for the building, we decided to upgrade our team of professionals.

The financing requirements for apartment buildings differed from those for houses. My existing mortgage broker was good at residential financing but did not have the qualifications to get us financing for an apartment building. We found another mortgage broker who specialized in apartment building financing.

We also found a real estate agent and lawyer who specialized in this area. The last thing we required was an on-site project manager to help direct the sub-trades.

I had a friend who was also a real estate investor and had the construction background, design skills and mindset we were looking for.

We had several meetings and all agreed that he would work with us on our project. However, instead of being paid a wage, we gave him equity in the property in lieu of a salary. We all decided that it was a great strategy since everyone would be motivated towards increasing the value and the overall profit of the project.

We brought him on as a minor shareholder in our company. He and I worked together in the building completing much of the renovation ourselves. For the skills that we did not possess, we hired out other trades such as an electrician, plumber, carpet installer, roofer and finish carpenter.

The reason that we did most of the renovation work ourselves, was to control the renovation costs as well as to see what it actually took to complete an apartment building renovation.

After injuring my hand on the project and experiencing the grueling amount of physical work required, we realized that we could not physically do most of the renovations if we wanted to continue to grow.

While we may have saved some money by physically renovating the building ourselves, the time it took to renovate eleven units was significant.

We found it would have been more effective to hire most of the trades to complete the work quicker and therefore reduce our large monthly holding costs. We decided that on the next property we would remain the general contractor and hire all the sub-trades.

After the renovations were complete on the eleven suite building, we achieved our new increased rent roll. With our higher rents, we had increased the value of the property. Therefore, we were able to refinance and take out almost all of the money we had invested for the down payment and renovations.

Aside from increasing the rent role from $4,200.00 per month to over $7,000.00 per month, the other benefit of the renovation was that our building required less maintenance. In effect, it cost less to operate each month.

Now we were on the prowl for the next project. We assumed that the money that we pulled out from refinancing the apartment building could be used for a down payment and renovation for another building.

However, between the time that we purchased the eleven suite building and renovated it, real estate prices had increased rapidly in our area. They had increased to a point where the rent we could generate would not make up for the higher price we would have to pay to purchase the next building.

It seemed that investors were scooping up apartment buildings so that they could convert the apartments into condominiums and sell the individual units for incredible profits.

If we wanted to continue buying apartment buildings and holding them as long term rentals, we would have to put down a much larger down payment and we would be unable to refinance and get our money out. The market had changed and we had to change with it.

Since we already had experience renovating an apartment building, all we had to do was learn the process of converting a building into individual condominiums. We did our research, learned everything we could about the conversion process and jumped into the game.

We purchased a twelve suite apartment building and converted it into individual units for resale. The whole project took eleven months to complete. It was a huge effort, we made several mistakes and in turn we learned a great deal. Yet with all the mistakes we made, we still realized a healthy profit.

At about the time that half of the condominiums were sold, my partner and I purchased a fifteen unit apartment building to convert next. The plan was to take what we had learned on the first condo conversion project and apply it to the new building.

That brings us to where we are today – in the midst of the renovations on our new building.

When I look back at the last nine years, I am amazed at how my life has changed. It's not that I am that smart, in fact, far from it. It was the hard work, sacrifices and perseverance that paid off. With focus, patience and determination, I have exceeded my expectations and goals.

I made a promise to myself many years ago. I vowed that if I ever had a family, they would not bear the financial hardships that my parents endured. I came through on that promise. I know that no matter what the future holds, my wife and my children will not have their lives uprooted for a lack of money. Knowing that they are financially secure gives me great pride and joy.

The vehicle I used to get there was real estate. In essence, I played the game of Monopoly in real life. I started with the green houses and then traded them in for the red apartment building.

So, now it's up to you as to what you are going to do. Are you going to sit on the sideline and watch, or are you going to get in the game and play? It's your move.

Regards,
Cam Acheson, Investor & Businessman

PS. I've know Paul M. Hecht going on 8 years now. A general comment I'll make is that some people talk a lot and do very little. Paul would be the exception to that.

The entire time that I've known him, he has always been a stand up fellow who does what he says he's going to do in the good times and in the bad times. He has always maintained his personal integrity and the highest of possible standards in terms of how he conducts himself.

In that regard, Paul is probably one the best people that I have worked with at this point in my real estate career.

Inquire About Paul's DVD Home Training,
Live Seminars & Mentoring at:

www.PAULMHECHT.com

Inquire About Paul's DVD Home Training,
Live Seminars & Mentoring at:

www.PAULMHECHT.com

Everyday Real Estate Millionaires™

Inquire About DVD Paul's Home Training,
Live Seminars & Mentoring at:

www.PAULMHECHT.com

~ 54 ~

STORY TWO

ROB & JOANNE
LIVING THE DREAM

"To accomplish great things, we must dream as well as act."

~ Anatole France

www.PAULMHECHT.com

As I stand by the stone fireplace in the living room of our custom built home overlooking the ocean, I have to pinch myself. I never imagined that it would actually happen. We are finally living our dream.

My husband Rob and I are retired now. We live on an island in the Pacific Ocean and the custom home we recently built is completely paid off. We have great health and financial investments that will outlast our lifetime. I realize now that all the hard work has paid off.

The island we live on is located just off the west coast, with a population of just over 10,000 residents. It is inhabited by local artists, musicians, farmers and retirees. The island is scattered with numerous quaint restaurants and shops. We have lived here for just over two years.

The summer months bring in many tourists which is great for our chocolate, fudge, soap and lotion business. I have been making soaps and hand lotions from goat's milk for many years. We added the fudge and chocolate products to our business when we moved to the island.

In fact, I just returned from studying at the Callebaut Chocolate Academy. I am now an official chocolatier.

(That should look good on my resume should I ever need a job again.)

We make our products during the week and then sell them at the farmers market on the weekends to the locals and tourists. We make enough from our summer sales to pay for most of our living expenses for the year.

Our move to the island was well worth it. We love it here. Our retirement lifestyle is very much what we imagined. We are very fortunate that we live in such a beautiful place and are able to do what we love.

So how were we able to start with nothing and retire in the place of our dreams?

Looking back now, it all probably started when I was in my thirties. I was living in a town of about 40,000 people. I was grooming animals (including show dogs) in a tiny 100 square foot space at the back of a veterinary clinic.

Soon I had built up a loyal clientele and found myself recommending different brands of pet food that worked well for the show dogs' coats and overall health.

I met Rob at a wedding. He was a construction foreman who ran several crews of carpenters. His father was a personnel manager for a distillery for many years and like my mother, his mother stayed home, raised the children and ran the household.

We both had previous broken marriages and weren't looking for a serious relationship. Initially we were friends. In fact, we really didn't think much of each other in the beginning, so we were always very honest as we weren't trying to impress each other. One thing lead to another and the relationship became more serious. So serious that we got married and bought our first home together. It's funny how life works sometimes.

We purchased a small two bedroom home back in the 1980's just before the decline in real estate values. We had saved enough for the down payment from both of our jobs. Rob and I were both self-employed so financing wasn't easy to obtain. We eventually found a lender who gave us a mortgage at approximately 15% interest. The payments were high but between both of our wages we managed.

We held onto that property for close to two years. At that point we were ready to move out of town onto a larger piece of land. We wanted to have some space to raise chickens, goats and other live stock.

At the same time that we began looking for some land, the local economy was not doing well. Real estate values had not increased for several years, interest rates hovered around 18% and many people took losses when they sold.

We had some friends who told us about a property for sale just outside of town that had a house with twenty four acres. It was owned by a couple who was about to lose their acreage to the bank. The husband had lost his job and they could no longer afford the mortgage payments. Their property had been on the market for almost six months. It was listed for $150,000.00 and they had not received any offers.

We arranged to see the property and thought it was perfect for us. The sellers had dug out a large hole in the ground right in front of the house to build a swimming pool. They ran out of money and did not complete the pool. It was an eye-sore to most buyers. To us, the home was perfect and we could fill in the hole quite easily.

If we paid full price, we also would have had a tough time making the payment. We offered them what we could afford - $110,000.00. We found out that that amount would not be enough to pay off their existing mortgage. We also found out what the balance of their existing mortgage was and offered them $118,000.00 to pay off their debt. They agreed.

I am sure we could have beaten them up over the $8,000.00 but that was not how we operated. They had lost enough already and we could afford the $118,000.00. It came down to humanity. For us, it's not always about the bottom line.

> **INVESTMENT TIP:**
>
> IF YOUR BANK HAS TURNED YOU DOWN FOR A MORTGAGE ON RENTAL PROPERTY, TRY ANOTHER LENDER. THERE ARE NUMEROUS LENDERS WHO SPECIALIZE IN RENTAL PROPERTIES AND WANT YOUR BUSINESS.

Since we were still self employed, we were unable to obtain conventional financing. Once again, we received a mortgage from a private lender at 18% interest. As challenging as that loan was, that wasn't the biggest hurdle we had.

We still owned the two bedroom house we were living in and real estate was not selling quickly. We couldn't hold on to two properties for very long or we would be in trouble too.

Since the value had not increased in the two years we owned it, selling it would have meant a financial loss. Realtor commissions and legal fees would have set us back approximately $10,000.00. We considered renting it out while we waited for the real estate market to come back.

Fortunately at the same time, we had some friends who wanted to buy a house but couldn't qualify at the banks either.

After several conversations, we agreed to let them buy the house with a small down payment and we would finance it for them. Because they were friends we made the payments very affordable and we let them get in with a very small down payment. Since it was a private sale, we did not pay any real estate commissions.

We moved to the acreage and our friends moved into our previous house. Shortly thereafter they had a change of heart and decided they could no longer afford it. They moved out and gave it back to us.

We sold it. We owned that property for three years. They lost their down payment and we lost about

$10,000.00 on the sale after realtor commissions and legal fees.

Even though we lost money, we had no regrets. We learned a great deal about owning property. We built up our credit and established ourselves as homeowners.

INVESTMENT TIP:

ALL REAL ESTATE AGREEMENTS (BIG OR SMALL) NEED TO BE IN WRITING SO THAT THERE ARE NO MISUNDERSTANDINGS. TO SAVE MONEY, WRITE OUT THE TERMS OF YOUR AGREEMENT AHEAD OF TIME AND THEN HAVE A LAWYER FINALIZE IT.

We also learned not to be so casual with friends about business. Just because they were friends, things still had to be done properly.

After that move, sale, loss of friends and sale again, we focused on our business. Rob and I decided to work together. We turned my grooming business and pet food referrals into a mid sized retail pet food business and grooming service. We named it the Barking Lot and ran it together for more than 28 years.

About three years before we sold it, we knew that if we wanted a chance of selling it for a good dollar, we had to make it as successful as possible.

Most Pet Food or for that matter, service businesses were difficult to sell since a large part of the value was in the "goodwill." The goodwill was the loyalty of the customer and if the new owner didn't treat the customer properly, the goodwill disappeared quickly. Therefore it was difficult to place a value on the business.

Fortunately, we were known in the pet industry as leaders for new products, knowledge and grooming. We were always bringing in the top lines of pet foods, health care products and grooming techniques. We treated our customers and employees like family.

With a little foresight, planning and effort, we eventually got the business to a point where it was attractive to a purchaser. The hard work paid off and we sold it fairly quickly for a healthy profit.

It was a huge relief to sell the business. We put 28 years of hard work and effort into that business. As much as we enjoyed the customers and staff, it was time to hand the business to someone else.

After we sold the business, we had time to think about our retirement and research where we wanted to live. At first, we were very hesitant to leave a town in which we had spent the past 35 years. It was a great big unknown for us. We hadn't moved in 35 years and we were at the age where a move would be very tiring.

We ended up purchasing two acres of land with an ocean view on an island - the property we live on today. Since we did not want to tie up too much of our own cash on the purchase, we asked the sellers if they would take a down payment and the balance would be paid off within twelve months. That gave us time to figure things out. They agreed and we made them two more payments before the land was transferred to us.

By purchasing the property in that manner, we avoided any financing costs associated with a mortgage or loan. Twelve months later the value of the land had increased more than 30%. We did all right on that one.

There was a period of approximately eighteen months between when we sold our business and eventually moved to the island. At that point, we were very concerned about what we should do with the nest egg that we received from the sale of our business. You see in the past, we had made some poor investment choices.

While we were still running our pet food business we were able to write off a large percentage of our personal expenses. That combined with the fact that we had a low cost of living, meant that we had a fare amount of disposable income during the later years of our business.

We used some of that income to invest in various investments. Unfortunately, we made several poor investment choices.

Initially we had bought goats, ostriches and other live stock. The challenge always hooked us, or me in particular, and always seemed so easy. At the end of the day, we never made any money in our livestock ventures. In fact, we lost more than we ever made.

Some of our other crazy get-rich-quick ideas lead us right into the hands of a true con artist. He had us invest into a pyramid scheme. I'm not talking about network marketing. I mean this guy was good. He was supposedly raising money to help children in our public school system. His wife was even a teacher and sat on the school board. He was offering 10% return per month. Wow, we wanted in!

Along with the rest of the people who fell for it, like sheep we invested some pretty good money. At first everyone was making money and then the payments stopped.

He was "robbing Peter to pay Paul." The case is still in the courts today and all the evidence (money) is gone. Apparently there was no trace of it. We knew we had lost it all once the phone calls and excuses started. We realized that if it sounded too good to be true, it probably was. We should have done our homework. We followed the heard and blindly invested.

INVESTMENT TIP:

IF AN INVESTMENT SEEMS TOO GOOD TO BE TRUE, IT PROBABLY IS. ALWAYS DO YOUR RESEARCH PRIOR TO INVESTING IN ANY VENTURE.

We also invested in mutual funds. Not a great choice for us either. We found them to be extremely impersonal. We did not like all the management fees, payout penalties, lack of control and overall low returns.

As a result of our poor investment choices, our confidence was affected for many years. We were not very comfortable about making investment decisions due to our previous track record. We did not want to lose our retirement nest egg, nor did we want to run out of money in our retirement years.

I did a lot of research and eventually found that real estate seemed to be the safest investment vehicle available to us. It was the most secure and tangible investment we could find. We felt that it was the safest place to invest our money without a large risk of losing it. We also wanted to control our own investments. We decided to put our money into rental or income real estate.

We didn't always know a lot about real estate. In fact, even owning real estate for over thirty years, we still didn't even know a good real estate investment if it hit us in the face. We knew people were making money with investment real estate. We just had to figure out how they were doing it and then do the same.

We educated ourselves extensively before investing again. We read many books, took courses and even hired a mentor to help us. The mentor helped us avoid costly mistakes and the time it would take for us to learn on our own. This really helped us with our fear about losing our money. We realized that the education was what we were lacking. With the education we could then make informed decisions. That gave us the confidence we needed.

We wanted to make sure that we fully understood all the concepts we were learning in the books and the mentor was someone with experience that we could talk to. We also wanted to learn ways to be hand-offs or passive in our real estate investments. We were past the point of picking up a hammer and cleaning toilets.

We decided to purchase an investment property ourselves so that we understood the ins and outs. It was very different than purchasing our own home. There were a lot more things to consider.

For example, did our rent cover all our expenses? If not, then we could be paying the difference. Would we hire and pay a property manager? Who would mow the lawn and water the grass? Was there a fee for garbage collection and who paid that? Who paid the utilities? How did we screen a tenant properly? How much rent could we charge? Was there rent control in our area and what did that mean to us as landlords? How did we evict a problematic tenant? These were all things we didn't have to consider with our own home. We had a lot to learn.

Because we wanted to be more hands-off with our investment real estate, our mentor introduced us to the idea of the rent-to-own and ran us through all the logistics and numbers. By investing in this manner, we could alleviate a large portion of the typical property management hassles.

The best part was that we would be able to help someone else into home ownership. The idea of giving someone a hand up instead of a hand out was what we had always believed in. It sounded like a great way to invest.

INVESTMENT TIP:

MAKING SURE THAT YOU CAN COLLECT ENOUGH RENT FROM YOUR RENTAL PROPERTY TO COVER ALL THE PROPERTY'S EXPENSES WILL ALLOW YOU TO KEEP YOUR RENTAL PROPERTY IN THE EVENT THAT YOU LOSE YOUR JOB.

Our mentor helped us figure out what type of property to buy and how to set up all the paperwork. We went on the hunt for a two or three bedroom starter home in a good area that a first time home owner would likely consider - nothing fancy as it had to be affordable for them. We weren't buying for us anymore.

We started by hiring a local real estate agent. Since our experience level wasn't that high and our self confidence was low, we did a few thing to overcome our own anxieties.

First off, we looked at about thirty houses before we were ready to buy one. With the education and insight from our mentor, we finally knew what a good deal looked like. We knew a good property at a good price when we saw it. We knew the market intimately and we established our end profit before we bought.

We also researched the area, neighborhoods, amenities and the local economy. We built our knowledge which gave us the confidence to buy.

We also wanted to cover our risks. Therefore we bought an entry level house where the rent would cover all our expenses and it wouldn't be a major burden if it was vacant. It was also attractive to a large segment of the population since it was affordable. We felt that it was a very safe purchase.

Furthermore, we hired a qualified property inspector to perform a home inspection. This kept us from fearing that the house would become a money pit.

Finding the right people or tenants was another risk. Our mentor showed us how to effectively screen tenants properly. Eventually we had to take an educated guess. We got as much knowledge as we could so that were prepared and could sleep at night.

We bought a three bedroom, two storey home with curb appeal, in a good neighborhood, close to amenities and schools. We screened our tenants and found a young couple who wanted to eventually own a home.

Because we were helping them get into home ownership, they helped us by taking care of the majority of the maintenance. They also signed a long term lease which took away any vacancy and advertising costs and time on our part.

We set up a monthly payment plan for the tenants to pay in addition to their rent. It was like a forced savings plan which they eventually used for their down payment. After twenty four months of renting and paying into the plan, they had enough saved up to buy the house.

It was a very positive experience knowing that we helped someone purchase their first home. We made just over 40% ROI on our money each year for two consecutive years. Not a bad profit for helping someone out and having very little management headaches ourselves.

INVESTMENT TIP:

IT IS POSSIBLE FOR RETIREES AND SELF EMPLOYED PEOPLE TO OBTAIN A MORTGAGE WITHOUT PROVING THEIR INCOME.

The process of educating ourselves, working with our mentor and purchasing the property took about ten months after the sale of our business.

Once we had set up the rent-to-own and the tenants were moved in, we moved to the island a few months later. We were a little hesitant about moving so far away from our investment property. However we had arranged to have a friend watch the property and our mentor told us that he was not far away either.

Before we could move to the island, we had to sell the acreage on which we lived. We listed the property for sale with a real estate agent who specialized in acreage property. Within thirty days, we had an offer for $550,000.00. That turned out much better than our previous home. In the offer we had included a term which allowed us to rent it back for up to three months so that we could take our time packing our belongings and saying our good-byes to friends. It really was a great offer and worked out well for us.

The people who purchased it from us subdivided the twenty four acres we had into four eight-acre lots. After the subdivision costs of approximately $50,000.00 they sold them all for just over $800,000.00 within a twelve month window. They made about $200,000.00. Good for them.

INVESTMENT TIP:

IF YOU PURCHASE LAND, CHECK WITH LOCAL CITY OFFICIALS TO SEE IF THE PROPERTY CAN BE SUB-DIVIDED.

We had a moving truck take most of our possessions over to the island. We drove our truck out to the island along with a trailer full of goats and other livestock. We must have looked like a bunch of hillbillies cruising along the highway in our twelve year old suburban.

Once we moved to the island, we bought a trailer to live in while we had our home built. Our driveway had a slope towards the trailer so we had to be very careful that we didn't slide down the side of the hill into our trailer during a downpour of rain. The construction of our home took approximately twelve months to complete.

INVESTMENT TIP:

YOU CAN USE YOUR RRSP, 401K or IRA TO INVEST IN REAL ESTATE THROUGH A SELF-DIRECTED ACCOUNT.

With the sales proceeds from our pet food store, we paid off the two acre lot on the island, used some money for the down payment on our rent-to-own investment property and paid off a large portion of the construction costs of our new home. From the proceeds of the sale of our 24 acre acreage, we had a sizable amount of cash to live on and invest.

With the money we brought in from the farmer's market sales, we had enough to cover the majority of our living expenses. Therefore we did not have to dip into our savings and could invest our money. Again, we chose real estate.

Since we did not want to have an active role in our real estate investments, our mentor showed us a few ways to invest so that we did not have to do any physical work, or incur any management hassles. In our case, we had some money to invest and did not want to be active in the day to day management and activities of a property.

From Rob's experience as a carpenter, he knew the amount of work a renovation took and therefore we needed someone else to do any work required. We wanted to take a more a passive role.

Our mentor explained that we could lend our money as a mortgage which would be secured by the property or we could invest with other people and share in the equity profits.

If we lent our money as a mortgage, we would receive a monthly interest payment every month just like a bank does. Our mentor explained that private investors often lent their money as a second position mortgage since the rate of return was typically higher than a first position mortgage. The amount of money required for a second mortgage was typically less than that of a first mortgage.

It was very common for a second mortgage monthly payment to be interest only. That meant that none of the principal got paid down and therefore it was very easy to calculate and track.

INVESTMENT TIP:

A JOINT VENTURE AGREEMENT IS TYPICALLY USED FOR A SPECIFIC, ONE-TIME PROJECT. THE JOINT VENTURE DOES NOT FILE FOR INCOME TAX. THE JOINT VENTURERS CLAIM THEIR SHARE (PROFIT OR LOSS) OF THE JOINT VENTURE PERSONALLY.

We invested almost half our investment money that way and at one point we were receiving almost $2,000.00 per month from the interest payments alone. With the income from the farmer's market and this additional interest income, we had more than enough to live very comfortably. This was a great way for us to receive monthly income.

Another way we learned to invest passively was to invest in other peoples active projects as a joint-venture partner. This way we could share in the equity and profit of a property. The only down side was that we would not receive any monthly income. However the returns were much higher at the end of those projects. We invested the other half of our investment money this way.

We invested this portion of our money with some bright young guys who were investing in rental properties. They were buying run down rental properties that had potential. They renovated the property, increased the rents and found good quality tenants.

We used our cash for the down payment and the renovations. Our partners found the property, did all the renovations, found good tenants and managed the property until we sold it.

Our agreement was to split the profits 50/50. We had a lawyer draw up the joint venture agreement.

Putting up money for a project did have risks. The risk we saw was putting our trust in the people we were investing with. If they didn't know what they were doing we would have been in a risky position.

To lessen our risk, we asked lots of questions and took our time finding the right joint venture partners. We made sure we knew who we were dealing with that time.

The plan was to own the property together for a few years and then sell it for a profit. The renovations had increased the property's value. Therefore we could refinance the property based on the increased value and get initial money back. This way we could buy more property and repeat the formula.

We sold the first joint venture property last year and received our first joint venture profit for just under $100,000.00! Our joint venture partner received the same amount also. We invested $112,000.00 and turned it into just over $210,000.00. It took 18 months from the time we bought the property to the time it was sold.

The return on cash that we received as joint-venture-partners turned out to be much higher than our return on cash from our mortgage investments. Since we had to wait until the sale was complete, the largest downside was that we did not receive any monthly payments to pay the monthly bills.

However, the mortgage investments paid the monthly bills. That was how we balanced our investment income with the growth of our capital.

After we refinanced the first joint venture property, we purchased a four-plex with the same guys and completed the same process. We still own the four-plex with our joint venture partners and are now in the process of refinancing the property to get our capital out. Once again, we invested the cash and they renovated the property. After the renovations, our new rent role was 60% higher than when we bought it. This was a result of the renovations as well as an increase in overall property values. The return was about the same as the first project.

We had a few rules about investing with others. First of all, we had to know the people very well and find out who they were. Then we found out which properties they had previously been involved in. Had they renovated before? Had they managed property and tenants before or was it their first project? We even viewed some of their previous projects to see the type of renovations they did. We asked what challenges they had and how they solved them. A dead give away for us was that if they said they never had any challenges and it worked out perfectly, then we knew they were not being honest. Honesty is mandatory for us.

We also wanted to know the downside to the property and the risks involved. Every property had a downside. Whether it was the location, current condition, size, quality or competition from other properties in the area, there was always a down side. If we were told there was "no risk," we always walked away.

For the most part, during our retirement, we were passive investors and did not get involved with the day-to-day management of tenants or renovations. We invested through joint ventures with other investors and lent our money as mortgages.

There were several younger people with a lot of knowledge about real estate who were willing to do the hands-on work. We invested the money and they did the work. It worked out very well for both parties.

Looking back now and reflecting on the events that lead us to where we are today, I realize that Rob and I are truly wealthy. To me that means that we are happy, healthy and living a life we love. We don't lay awake at night worrying about our finances. We have our business and real estate investments to thank. While we are still cautious with our money, we know that we have enough for the rest of our lives. In the event that we lost it or ran out, we would simply make more. No one can take away our knowledge or zest for life. It's as simple as that.

Respectfully,
Joanne and Rob, Retirees

PS. For the young people out there who are interested, here are our words of wisdom to you. These "words of wisdom" have taken many years to create and have caused a few grey hairs. Use the grey hairs wisely please.

1. Work hard at whatever you do.

2. Get a small business for the tax write offs.

3. Learn a skill or trade at a job. Then use the skills for your own business.

4. Start investing as young as possible. You can never buy back time.

5. Become educated in real estate. Read lots of books, take courses, research the area you want to invest in and then start investing.

6. Be patient and don't take the first deal. There's always another one.

7. Get a mentor if you have the means.

8. Buy a house with a rental income or suite or get roommates to help pay the mortgage. Remember

that the situation need not be permanent. However, it's a great way to get started.

9. Don't work for 40 – 50 years and then drop dead. Life is a balance. Enjoy it along the way.

10. Do not hoard for retirement, there is always more.

11. You also can't just live for today. The government will not pay for your retirement.

12. If you don't have the cash, don't buy it (except for real estate.)

13. Live within your means.

14. Work on your credit rating and protect it.

15. Do something you love and invest the money.

16. Don't fall for the get-rich-quick schemes. It takes time and effort to build wealth properly.

17. Give people a hand up, not a hand out.

18. Always look for a way for both parties to benefit in a negotiation.

19. Take time to celebrate your victories – big or small.

20. If you've done your due diligence, then get off the fence and take the leap of faith.

21. Finally, find out what makes you truly happy. You don't have to spend a lot to be happy.

We have always enjoyed providing value to others. Doing a good job and being recognized for the value we provided made us happy. It was really that simple for us. What makes you happy?

Good luck and we hope to see you on the island some day!

PSS. We'd always been interested in real estate but our experience was limited to owning our own home, not investment real estate. As we had decided to check out investing in real estate and realized that we needed to educate ourselves; that led us to Paul M. Hecht who we met 7 years ago.

We took his real estate mentoring program which was very thorough and easy to understand. With his on-

going coaching and mentoring, we gained the confidence to do this.

Paul is honest, has integrity and his advice is sound and thorough. He taught us how to do well in all real estate markets, whether up or down, if you buy right and know your exit plan.

Today, we continue to invest in real estate with his guidance. We wouldn't be in the positive financial position we are today and able to enjoy our retirement without his training and mentorship.

Inquire About Paul's DVD Home Training,
Live Seminars & Mentoring at:

www.PAULMHECHT.com

~ 84 ~

Inquire About Paul's DVD Home Training,
Live Seminars & Mentoring at:

www.PAULMHECHT.com

~ 85 ~

Inquire About Paul's DVD Home Training,
Live Seminars & Mentoring at:

www.PAULMHECHT.com

STORY THREE

DEAN

IT'S ALL ABOUT THE REASON

"If you can dream it, you can do it."

~ Walt Disney

www.PAULMHECHT.com

My story is very simple. I made a lot of money with real estate. Did I like doing it? Sure. While some of it was hard work, for the most part I quite enjoyed myself. Do I like the money? Of course, who wouldn't? But here's the real question. Do I like what the money can provide? Absolutely. You see, to me, real estate was and is a means to an end.

Anyone who knows me knows what is really important to me. It's not money, expensive cars or flashy clothes – it's my family. It's my wife, our kids, our extended family and close friends. They are what really matter to me. What is also important to me is the life that we, as a family, can lead as a result of our real estate success.

Even before I was married and had children, I had an image of what my ideal life would look like. I always knew that I wanted to control my own future and did not want to answer to anyone else. I knew that I wanted freedom and choice. I just wasn't sure how I would get there.

When I met my wife and started having children, we knew that we wanted to follow their lead and provide them with every possible opportunity. We knew that we wanted to be a constant presence in their lives, to be the very best parents and to be there for them every step of the way. We wanted our children to experience life to the fullest and for all of us to be a family in every sense of the word. In essence, we wanted to give our children a head start in life so that for them there would be no limits.

However at that time in my life, before I started investing in real estate, I was working a full time job with a set salary. I knew that if I was to turn that vision into reality, it would require more commitment, time

INVESTMENT TIP:

IF YOU WORK AS A TEAM WITH EITHER A SPOUSE OR PARTNER TOWARDS THE SAME GOALS, YOU HAVE AN AUTOMATIC SUPPORT SYSTEM.

and money than my job would provide.

Let me share with you how I went from a place of discontent to living the incredible life that my wife and I envisioned for ourselves and for our family – all with the help of real estate.

My background was in computer consulting. At the time, the large consulting firm that I worked for sold software and IT services to oil and gas companies. I worked with high tech 3-D software on a computer

~ 89 ~

screen that stood ten feet tall by fourteen feet wide to view underground oil wells. At the end of the day, I was just a high-tech grunt. As long as I was putting in billable hours the company was making money and they were happy. If I wasn't working, I was worth nothing to the company. The endless treadmill was tiring.

In my line of work the only way I could get advances in pay was to move into middle-management, go overseas, or do a lateral move to a different company.

When the company I was working for looked at their margins and last year they produced a 15% profit for their shareholders, this year they needed a 17% - 18% profit to keep shareholders happy.

Layoffs were predictable. Middle management was always the first to go, or the so called "fat." Upper management couldn't be fired and the workers were needed to do the work. Middle management was the easiest target to cut first and therefore not the "move up" I was looking for.

The other alternative of going overseas or being transferred to another country would take both my wife and I away from our roots and family. Lateral moves within the industry seemed like the only way that made any sense.

However, small raises and adding another company to my resume still weren't going to create the lifestyle that I wanted for my family. I decided it was time to make it on my own terms. I could only blame other people so long before I realized that if I wanted my life to change, I would have to make the changes.

Around the time that my wife was pregnant with our second child, we started seriously discussing how to get out of the daily grind, take control of our financial future and live the life we truly desired.

I had been reading many books at the time on finance, wealth and success as well as several business biographies. A quote in one of the books I had read stood out very distinctly in my mind. It was a quote by Andrew Carnegie who said, "More money has been made in real estate than all industrial investments combined." To me that statement was extremely powerful. I thought to myself – why not start there.

Coincidentally, around the same time, I stumbled upon a one day workshop about business, success and real estate. It was open to the public, so I decided to attend.

At the workshop, there were several presenters who discussed various topics such as starting a small business, network marketing and various investment opportunities. The presenter that piqued my interest was one who spoke about investing in real estate. The part that really got me interested was that their company offered a mentoring program to help people get started. I spoke with the presenter afterwards and we made an appointment to meet later that week

INVESTMENT TIP:

YOU CAN FIND LOCAL INVESTMENT CLUBS ONLINE. TO FIND INVESTMENT SEMINARS, LOOK IN THE BUSINESS SECTION AND CLASSIFIEDS OF YOUR LOCAL PAPER.

When I arrived home, I told my wife about the workshop and the real estate mentoring program. Together, we attended the scheduled appointment, asked numerous questions and received a great deal of information about the program. With the information in hand, we spent some time determining our next step.

The first thing my wife and I did was agree that we both wanted to take control of our financial future and that real estate would be our vehicle to wealth. Real estate seemed to be the quickest and safest way. It was the most proven over time and had more advantages than any other investment we researched.

Other than purchasing their own home, my parents were always afraid to invest in real estate. It was out of their comfort zone. We had to get out of our comfort zone and push our boundaries if we wanted things to change for us. No one was going to make us wealthy other than ourselves.

The second thing we agreed to do was to do it together as a team and support each other in our decisions. My wife's attitude was, and still is, that if something went wrong and the real estate didn't work out, then I could go and get another job. If that was the worst case scenario, then what did we have to lose?

The third thing we realized was that to do it properly, we had to get educated. We realized that we could obtain our education a few different ways. We could either learn on our own, or we could hire someone to help us.

We liked the idea of having someone help us with such a daunting task. If we wanted to invest properly, save time and avoid costly mistakes, we would benefit from a mentor.

In real estate if we made a mistake it would be very easy to lose thousands, if not tens of thousands of dollars. We felt that a mentor would help point us in the right direction from the start.

INVESTMENT TIP:

WHEN SEEKING OUT A MENTOR, FIND SOMEONE WHO HAS DONE WHAT YOU WANT TO DO. INTERVIEW THEM AND ASK FOR REFERENCES.

We decided to hire a mentor and coughed up a good chunk of money to pay for his services. I realized that if I wanted real estate to support me and my family, I had to get serious and treat the mentorship as a real education similar to that of going to college or university. After all, if I could make the kinds of profits that real estate offered, wasn't that worth it? I was going to find out; it was just a matter of when.

The perfect opportunity presented itself after the birth of our second child. I decided to make good use of my employer's optional paternal leave program and informed my boss that I was going to take a month of unpaid leave to be at home with my family.

During my month off, my wife and I immersed ourselves in real estate. Through our mentor's guidance, we learned numerous strategies and techniques to profit from real estate that we hadn't even known existed. We thought that to get into real estate, you either bought a property, rented it out and became a landlord or, you bought a property, fixed it up and sold it. We were wrong.

With so many options we didn't know where to start. What we really discovered was that we had to learn as much as we could and then take action.

Our mentor told us that we couldn't do it all at once or we would get overloaded and end up with "analysis paralysis." He said that you eat an elephant one bite at a time. That calmed us down. He assured us to just take one step at a time and then asked us to write down our goals and our strategy would fall into place.

We broke down our goals into Financial, Personal, and Toys. Financial goals were things like no debt by a certain date, bringing in a certain amount of income per month or annually, or passive income of X, a net worth of Y and the like.

The personal goals included things like losing ten pounds by a certain date, spending more time with my kids, volunteering with a charity, giving back to the community, having a certain night out with my wife, etc.

Then the fun stuff was the toy goals. That included cars, trips, vacations, airplanes, boats, jewelry, etc.

We had to get very specific about our goals and break them down into one year, three year and five year goals in each category. We then picked the top 3 goals in each category and attached specific dates to them, along with any details.

Our mentor told us that if we did not hit the dates or have the exact amount of net worth we wrote down, or the exact goal we wanted, not to beat ourselves up. Having goals gave us focus and clarity on what we wanted. The focus and clarity was more important than the specifics of the goals. He said we would be amazed at how close the specifics of the goal would be on the date we noted. The focus allowed us to be clear on what we wanted.

He also suggested we use visualization tools to help us visualize our goals. We printed pictures off the internet of what we wanted. For example, I printed off my sports car and my wife printed out her SUV. We printed out our ideal vacation home and pictures of real estate that we wanted to own since our real estate was going to be the means to achieving our goals.

Once we completed our goals separately, we looked at each other's goals and found that we had many similar goals. One of those goals was to transition out of my job within two to three years.

INVESTMENT TIP:

A VISION BOARD ALLOWS YOU TO BECOME MORE FOCUSSED ON THE REASON(S) YOU ARE INVESTING.

The reality of being self-employed was very motivating for me as it was completely up to us to make it happen. There was no one else to blame but ourselves.

So much had happened during my month off. About a week after I returned back to work, our "big bang" occurred. One night while I was in a deep sleep, my wife woke me up in bed. I thought that it was my lucky night but she had other plans. She looked me straight in the eyes and said, "Get up, you're quitting your job today." I looked over at the clock - it was 4:00 am. She had been up all night thinking about how we could do this full time.

After reviewing our finances and balance sheet, she had been trying to figure out how we could be full time real estate investors. Thankfully for me, it finally hit her at 4:00 am in the morning. She came up with a plan for me to quit my job and go full time with real estate.

After about two days of contemplating the pros and cons, and reviewing our financial situation, we were ready to go for it.

As I was standing at the photocopier at work, I took a moment to reflect as my resignation letter slid onto the tray. I then gave my notice. Everyone at work was shocked and that's when I started to think "Yikes, what have I done?"

Having the courage to quit my steady income and go on my own was a real test in itself. All I had to do was think about my parent's fear which kept them in their comfort zone. We had nothing to lose and everything to gain. We pushed through our major comfort zone and security boundaries.

Now please understand, we did not have a lot of money, but we did have enough to live on for about six months before we would need a cash infusion. We also had a back up plan that if worse came to worst, I could either get another job or we could sell our home. We went for it and needed some cash from our real estate investments before our six months was up.

Two days before I was about to leave, my boss asked me into his office. He told me that if I ever needed another job, I would always be welcomed back. It was nice to know that I was not only leaving on my own terms, I was also leaving on good terms.

It was June 19, 2002 — my final day at work. At the end of the day, I stood in the doorway with the mental snapshot of my office to remind myself I'd never have to see it again. I closed the door behind me and quietly left the building for the last time. I never said a word to anyone - I just left, knowing that I was on my way.

Thankfully, just before I quit my job, we had purchased a home for ourselves that would accommodate our future needs. Instead of putting down a large down payment, we put down a small down payment and obtained a larger mortgage. This freed up some cash to invest.

When we bought our newest primary residence for $250,000.00, we put down only 5% ($12,500.00). Since we had over $60,000.00 in profit from our previous home, we had $45,000.00 cash that we put in the bank. With our six months of savings plus this new cash, we actually had some money to invest.

My wife had a retirement plan for $30,000.00 that she cashed in also. Since she was not working, she paid very little income tax to cash in her retirement account.

Ready to start our new venture, our mentor suggested we write down a list of our financial resources in order to find out what we could utilize. In other words how much cash did we have, could we qualify for loans, did we have other property whose equity we could use to buy more, did we have other investments such as mutual funds, stocks, bonds and the like that we could sell to raise money.

We wrote down a list of the resources we had along with the skills we had. That was a great exercise and it really opened our eyes.

Our mentor pointed out that our largest and most valuable resource was the time we had. With both of us home, we had time to get to know the market and focus primarily on real estate.

I also asked friends, family and business associates if they wanted to invest into our properties. One friend gave us the name of an associate he knew who would lend his money as second mortgages on properties that we wanted to purchase. This would allow us to buy properties with less cash upfront since he would provide us with second mortgages from his retirement account.

INVESTMENT TIP:

PERSONAL RESOURCES INCLUDE MONEY, ABILITY TO QUALIFY FOR FINANCING, EQUITY, TIME, SKILLS AND ABILITIES, SPECIALIZED KNOWLEDGE, CONTACTS, TRADE ASSOCIATIONS, PEOPLE SKILLS AND MANAGEMENT ABILITY.

Then our mentor told us we would need some people on our team to help us do this faster and properly. He said real estate was like baseball. You need the pitcher, the catcher, base men plus the fielders and of course the coach. Everyone has a position. If one is weak, the ball will go through and the whole team will feel it.

INVESTMENT TIP:

WHEN BUILDING YOUR INVESTMENT TEAM OF PROFESSIONALS, FIND THOSE WHO SPECIALIZE IN WORKING WITH INVESTORS. ASK THEM TO GIVE YOU AN EXAMPLE OF THE TYPES OF INVESTORS THEY HAVE WORKED WITH.

Your real estate investment team can include a lawyer, a realtor, banker or mortgage broker, appraiser, inspector, bookkeeper, accountant, contractor, and property manager. Depending on the size and complexity, you may need a structural engineer, environmental engineer, architect, surveyor and project manager. He recommended we put together a list of people with names that we would need on our team.

We found a real estate lawyer, mortgage broker who worked with investors, a good inspector and an accountant. After searching for almost four months, we finally found a realtor with the same mindset as us who understood investment property.

Surprisingly, the real estate agent was the toughest person to find on our team. We found that most agents did not understand investment property. They understood residential valuation, marketing and contracts but not real estate as an investment. It was like we were speaking different languages.

Then our mentor explained that most real estate agents do not fully understand real estate as an investment, unless they take additional training. He suggested we ask the potential agent if they had taken any additional investment training or even better, if they owned any investment real estate themselves.

We used his suggested approach and found an agent who owned a few rental properties himself. He was much more effective than any other agent with whom we had previously spoken. Working with someone who understood what we were looking for was very exciting and very efficient for us. Within a few weeks, our new agent had located some excellent opportunities.

We looked at several properties over a period of a few weeks before picking the first target. We liked the idea of having very little property management and headaches and therefore we picked the "lease option/ rent-to-own" strategy.

We located a three-bedroom town home for $135,000.00. At the time, that was considered entry level pricing in our city. The property was in good condition and in a good family neighborhood.

We made an offer and our offer was accepted. For the next three hours, I was so afraid that we had just made the biggest mistake of our lives. I imagined all the different things that could go wrong and all the mistakes that we could make. My fear of the house caving in on itself from structural damage along with an old rotten leaky roof, old furnace and old wiring was just the start of my worries. Tenants certainly would not pay rent and I would spend my time tracking them down like a lion. Then they would get upset and burn down the house. That was the icing on the cake.

I was certain we were going to lose the property which would result in us losing our own home. Then I would have to go back to work broke, and I would be a failure living on the street. I got so upset and worried that I actually became physically ill!

The only thing I could think of was to phone my mentor. I told him what had happened and that I wanted to know how I could get out of the contract immediately.

He asked me one thing that changed my whole attitude immediately. He asked, "What do the numbers tell you?" I told him they looked very good. We then reviewed all the numbers together.

He then asked if I had conditions in the offer like he told us to do. I told him that the offer was subject to us completing a home inspection that was satisfactory to us as well as our ability to take over the existing financing.

He then reminded me that the home inspection would identify any major problems with the house. If there was something major identified, we could always renegotiate to have the items repaired or walk away from the contract.

As far as tenants went, he told us how to screen them and what questions to ask. After we had asked the right questions, checked their credit and their references, we'd know who the good tenants were. The screening process eliminated more than 90% of the bad tenants.

Then he told me to take it one step at a time and asked if I was still worried. I told him that I didn't know any more. We had a good laugh. He told me that it was normal to worry. We took it one step at a time and bought the property.

We took possession on March 31 and the new tenants started their occupancy on April 1. No holding costs for us and we were cash flow positive from day one.

We gave the tenants the option to purchase the property after twenty four months for $154,000.00. Again, they took care of all the maintenance and we had zero vacancy, minimal management and no selling commissions.

The first set of tenants moved out after eight months as they decided they did not want to purchase the property after all. They had put up $3,000.00 for the option, which was non-refundable.

We found our next set of tenants and since the market had gone up, we gave the new tenants the option to purchase the property for $180,000.00 after twenty four months. They too put up $3,500.00 (non-refundable) for the option. After only four months, the husband was called to duty and transferred back to England within thirty days.

Again we advertised the property as a rent-to-own. This time the new tenants could purchase the property for $204,000.00. Finally, twenty four months later, our latest tenants bought the property. At that point it was worth approximately $220,000.00 so they bought below market value.

With mortgage pay down and the two non-refundable option deposits we had received, that deal put over $90,000.00 in our pocket. Initially, we had financed 85% of the purchase price with a mortgage and we put down 15%. We had another $1,500.00 in closing costs.

It was 36 months from start to finish. Our ROI (Return on Investment) was over 400%. Wow. If you break that down annually, it comes out to 130% ROI per year for three consecutive years. Not bad for beginners.

INVESTMENT TIP:

A PRE-FORECLOSURE IS WHEN THE BANK HAS SENT THE OWNER A DEMAND LETTER. THE OWNER STILL HAS CONTROL. A FORECLOSURE IS WHEN THE BANK HAS TAKEN THE PROPERTY. AT THAT POINT YOU CAN ONLY DEAL WITH THE BANK.

The next property we purchased was a foreclosure for $167,000.00. We planned on renovating the property and then selling it on the market for a profit. We used our line of credit to pay for the renovations, thinking that when the property sold, the line of credit would be paid off.

At the end of the renovation, we put the property on the market and our nightmare began. The property did not sell. The line of credit was not paid off.

After almost ninety days, we finally received an offer for what we had purchased the property at initially. If we sold the property for that price, we would have lost our renovation costs, holding costs, our time and labor, and the real estate commission costs for a total loss of $20,000.00. That's when we called our mentor again.

He ran through all our costs, expenses and projected loss with us on the phone. Then he asked us what other strategy we could use on this property. Being all flustered as the offer was only open for one more hour, I thought he was crazy as we had to deal with the offer first. We didn't have time to think about other options.

Then he told me to slow down and take a breath. He continued to remind us that we had a renovated three bedroom house at entry-level pricing in a good neighborhood. He then asked us again: what other strategy can you use?

Immediately I thought of a lease option. He told me to run the numbers and call him back in ten minutes. So we did.

We realized that we could sell the property on a rent-to-own and have someone pay $208,000.00 in twenty four months and the rent we could generate from the property would cover all our monthly costs.

I phoned him back, and gave him the information. He then summarized by saying we could make approximately $40,000.00 in twenty four months by using a different strategy or we could lose $20,000.00 that day. He went on to say something I'll never forget. He said "It's always better to defer your profit than to take a loss today." I've never forgotten that phrase.

He also asked us how long it would take to make back our $20,000.00 loss?

Then he asked if I had calculated my ROI. Initially, we took over the existing financing and put down $18,000.00 for the down payment. Then we spent about $7,500.00 on renovations and $2,500.00 on carrying costs for a total of $28,000.00. We realized we would have a 142% ROI in 24 months or put another way, 71% per year for two consecutive years. I thanked him and hung up the phone.

We rejected the offer, took the property off the market and cancelled our listing agreement. Then we advertised the property as a rent-to-own. Within three weeks, we found a tenant who took the option for $208,000.00 in twenty four months and put up a $5,000.00 (non-refundable) option deposit. That property closed exactly twenty four months later for $208,000.00.

Had we accepted the initial offer, we would have lost approximately $20,000.00 plus our time and effort. It's not that the market changed, we just underestimated our costs and marketability.

Instead, by using a different strategy, we ended up with a 142% return on our money. Knowing the different strategies allowed us to turn what could have been a disaster into a success. In addition to everything we had learned, this was where our mentor paid off.

The only downside to holding the property for twenty four months was that the line of credit we used to pay for the renovations was not paid off. Nor did we have the profit to use for living expenses or further investments.

In the meantime, once we had that lease option in place, we helped my parents purchase a rental property and we managed it for them. After three years the market took a big jump in values and they ended up selling it for $100,000.00 more than they paid for it. We didn't partner with them. We simply helped them get into the market and managed the tenants for them.

While we were waiting for our real estate profits to come to fruition, and since we had invested all of our money, we had two pressing issues. The first was that we needed some money to cover our living expenses and pay our creditors. The second was that we needed to get creative regarding our real estate investments. With all of our money invested, how did we continue to invest?

Our solution to our first issue was very short term, but it got us through. We used more credit to put food on the table and cover our living expenses. While this resolution was not ideal, it was the only way we could see to get by at that point.

However, within a few months we had creditors calling. We had missed a few credit card payments and we were falling behind. The financial stress tested our resolve. It forced us to re-evaluate what was really important in our lives.

Through much soul searching, we realized that we would not accomplish our goals with a regular job and decided to do whatever it took in order to provide the life we wanted for our family. The faith in knowing that we were investing for the right reasons

INVESTMENT TIP:

YOU MAY BE ABLE TO "FLIP" PROPERTIES QUICKER BY OFFERING SELLER FINANCING.

was what kept us going. We knew that if we did not give up, we would come out on top.

With our financial situation in dire straights, we decided to sell our minivan for $7,000.00 and bought another one for $3,000.00. We used the cash to buy groceries, pay our mortgage and had enough to pay the bills and our creditors for that month.

Thirty days later we received an income tax refund. It was just enough to get us through for another month. We were just getting by.

Meanwhile, we still had our second issue to resolve. We knew that we needed to continue investing in real estate, but with no income and no cash, we needed to be resourceful.

We decided to partner with another investor that we had known for some time. He was in a similar situation financially and thought that if we combined our efforts, we could offer rent-to-owns to people who wanted to get into home ownership. With our limited financial resources, he suggested we try sandwich lease options.

At the time that we were getting into sandwich lease options, the rental market was slow, with many vacancies. There were numerous rentals for tenants to choose from so it was difficult for landlords to attract tenants. Landlords either had to renovate their units, lower the rental price or offer tenant incentives.

Our plan was to approach landlords about solving their problems by signing a two-year lease with them if we had the option to purchase their property within twenty four months. We would also take care of all the property maintenance for them. This gave landlords zero vacancies for two years plus limited maintenance. We solved their problems.

In our contract we had the right to sublease the property. We would then advertise the same property as a rent-to-own to attract sub-tenants. Those tenants would then rent the property from us. We had an option to purchase the property from the landlord at one price. We then gave the sub-tenants an option to purchase the property at a higher price. Therefore we would keep the difference between the two rental amounts, as well as the difference between the two option amounts. We became the middlemen - thus the term sandwich lease option.

Yet, since we both needed some quick cash, we decided we would flip a few properties at the same time we were setting up our sandwich lease options.

As it turned out, a couple with three school children came to view our first sandwich lease option property. Their children's school had re-designated who could attend the school. Their home was located outside the new boundary. Therefore they needed to move so that their children could still attend their desired school.

We met them and realized that if they sold their home with a realtor they would lose money. To start with, they did not have much equity in the property. Between realtor fees and a large payout penalty to discharge their existing mortgage, they were going to lose about $12,000.00.

We figured out a way to purchase the property from them, give them $8,000.00 cash and take over their existing financing. To them, it was better than losing $12,000.00 and going through the hassles of showing their property and selling with a realtor. They accepted our offer.

As we were planning to flip the property, the $8,000.00 would be paid to them when we had re-sold it.

We then immediately advertised the property for sale and offered seller financing with a low down payment to a new buyer. We made a profit of $17,000.00. That helped out with our cash crunch at home.

In the meantime, we tried to find a home for the sellers to move into. Since they did not have enough money for a down payment, a conventional purchase was not feasible. They decided to try our rent-to-own model. While this option wasn't perfect, it did give them the opportunity to work towards home ownership again.

We had the sellers view our first rent-to-own property, but it was located outside of their school boundary and therefore did not meet their requirements. However, we set up a second sandwich lease option property and offered them the property on a rent-to-own basis. It was located within their school boundary - just one block from the school they wanted their children to attend. Their children could walk to school. They took it.

The first sandwich lease option property was a three bedroom bungalow in a good neighborhood, by the local university. That property was initially listed for sale with a real estate agent who was also advertising it as a rental at the same time. The asking price was $219,000.00 and the rent was $1,000.00 per month.

We agreed to purchase the home for $214,000.00 on a twenty four month option. In the meantime we would pay $1,000.00 per month in rent. The sellers also agreed to paint the interior of the property since it was a little run down. With a fresh coat of paint, we offered the property as a rent-to-own.

We found a tenant to sublease the property and gave them an option to purchase the property for $251,000.00 in twenty four months. In the interim, they agreed to pay $1,250.00 per month in rent to us. We were then paying $1,000.00 to our landlord.

Since we had invested only $1,000.00 of our own cash (for security deposit) our return on our money was enormous. The best part about that deal was the minimal up-front cash and not having to qualify for any loans. We simply arranged the deal and took the difference between the two contracts. After twenty four months, we had made just over $40,000.00.

Our tenants were outstanding and we had no problems whatsoever with them. They were extremely happy with their purchase. At the time they exercised their option, the property was worth close to $300,000.00. They had almost $50,000.00 in equity when they bought it!

We then found another landlord who turned out to be a stockbroker. We approached him about renting his revenue property for two years if we had an option to buy it in the future. Since he was a stockbroker, he completely understood options. After some negotiation, he agreed.

The only difference this time was that this landlord wanted an appreciation rate on his property whereas the previous landlord just wanted someone to rent or buy the property to cover their monthly costs. They didn't care about any future increase in value.

Once we had this one in place, the stockbroker then approached us about buying another property and doing the same thing. We would locate an ideal property together. He would buy it and we would rent it from him with an option to buy it in the future. We would then re-rent the property to someone else and give them an option at a higher price than we had. It worked out great.

We decided to use that formula and had other investors purchase more properties. We would rent the properties from our investors and then re-rent them to other people. It was great for our investors since they had no management, vacancies, tenant hassles and maintenance. We did it all for them. In return we received an option on the property without using any of our own money or qualifying.

In the meantime, while we worked on the rent-to-owns, my partner and I continued to flip properties quickly to make some cash. The profits that we made from the flips were used to pay our living expenses.

We then expanded our business to include pre-foreclosures as another source for acquiring additional properties. We targeted people who were behind on their mortgage payments and needed to get out of their financial problems quickly.

Many people had the perception that we were like vultures who took advantage of these people. It was actually quite the opposite.

First of all, we did not cause the problem. The owners got themselves into their situation. For those homeowners, they would lose their house to the bank and ruin their credit rating for many years by having a foreclosure on their credit record. To most people, having someone take that type of stress away was a huge relief.

How we dealt with people in this situation was vital. Don't get me wrong, there were some investors who used scare tactics to frighten people into selling them their home. We did not approach people that way. We educated people about the foreclosure process and laid out several options that were available to them. We truly tried to help people understand that they had choices. It was up to them to decide.

Of the properties that we did purchase, we bought all of them below market value, but by no means did we get them at forty or fifty percent of their value, or even close to it. For example, we purchased a home on the golf course for $340,000.00. At the time it was worth $375,000.00. That's 90% of its market value.

We saved people's credit rating so that they could start again faster than if they had a foreclosure on their credit record. We did not pressure anyone into selling their homes to us and in fact many didn't. Quite a few homes went back to the bank and were sold to the general public.

> **INVESTMENT TIP:**
>
> **HAVING MULITPLE WAYS TO FIND PROFITABLE DEALS ALLOWS YOU TO BE SELECTIVE AND CHOOSE THE VERY BEST INVESTMENTS.**

Once we bought a property, sometimes the previous owners would rent the property until they found another place to live. Occasionally we would give the previous owners an option to buy the property back in the future as long as they made all their rent payments.

In essence we gave them a second chance. Whenever we did this we made it very clear that there was no third chance. This was their last chance.

We continued this process until we had acquired twelve properties within eighteen months through either sandwich lease options or pre-foreclosures.

Seven out of the twelve tenants exercised their option and purchased the property as agreed. Four tenants walked away from their option all together and we had to evict one. We sold three of the properties on the market and did quite well as the property's value had increased. We kept two properties as rentals.

After purchasing the initial twelve properties, we continued to purchase additional properties with other investors. Those properties were purchased with the intention of being held as long term rentals. We continue to hold most of those properties today.

So what have I learned through all of this that I can share with you?

Number One: Make sure your financial house is in order before you start your own business. If you're not sure, get professional advice. In the beginning, we had some days where we felt great about our decisions and other days we would panic about how the bills were going to get paid. Make sure you're honest with yourself about your situation, your monthly cost of living and your bills.

The biggest challenge we had starting out was in not knowing when the next deal was coming. This made it extremely difficult in trying to manage our finances and pay the bills. In the beginning it seemed to be feast or famine. Every business has cash flow problems - real estate had them too. However, real estate also had bonuses. The consistency of a regular paycheck was nonexistent.

Number Two: Don't quit your job too early. To be honest with you, I don't know if I would have done it that way again. I love being self-employed and I love the flexibility of my own time but we did create cash flow challenges and limited our ability to qualify for financing by not having a job.

Looking back now, the only thing I would have done differently is that I would not have quit my job so quickly. That would have been a safer route to take.

However, our mentor said that we all have lessons to learn and this was probably the quickest way for me to learn one of mine. He told me that when I quit my job, I was a procrastinator and still had the mindset of relying on other people for my income. I might not have received my self reliance had I not quit my job and realized for myself that I could survive on my own.

As he said, "If you do not learn it, it will eventually teach you." I guess we learned quickly. We learned that by experiencing it ourselves, it only made us stronger.

We couldn't learn how to drive or be self-employed or become a parent by reading a book. We had to experience it for ourselves to truly understand.

We worked extremely hard in the beginning and it paid off in the end. For the first two years we often worked days, evenings and weekends. Our theory was, "We can either play now and pay later or, pay now and play later." I'd rather work now while I still can so that I can enjoy the rest of my life and not have to worry about the future. And that is just what we did.

If there are any words of advice that we would offer, they would be - always maintain your integrity. This should go without saying. If you do not feel comfortable with a purchase, sale, business agreement or arrangement, do not proceed. There's no amount of money worth jeopardizing ones reputation or integrity. You need to be able to sleep at night.

Finally, have fun. Always, always, always! If it's not fun, you're not going to do it. Sometimes you will have to make it fun and some days you will have to persevere through the challenging times to find the light at the end of the tunnel.

My partner and I would often laugh at some of the crazy deals we would come across or put together. We had lots of fun and laughed hysterically many times.

With a little more time on my hands now, I have decided to offer consulting services three days a week to some of the oil and gas companies where I live. In three days of consulting, I now earn almost twice what I did when I was an employee full time. The money I make from my job is what we use to pay the bills. The money we make from our real estate investments is how we build our net worth for our retirement and security.

My life and the lives of my family are much different now because of real estate. I own several investment properties today and continue to grow my net worth. I have cash in the bank and all our bills are paid on time and in full.

We have also taken some incredible family vacations recently. Our success with our real estate investments has allowed us to take our children to parts of the world that they would have otherwise only read about in books or seen on television. We are so grateful to provide our children with these experiences.

I am also extremely thankful for my wife's support, dedication, perseverance and kick in the pants when I needed it. Because of her and our hard work together, we are now in control of our time and we make our own decisions. We are a strong family and try to instill strong morals and values in our children so they too can be self-reliant in their own lives.

We certainly look at things differently now and already see it in our children. Our hope for them is that they will do whatever they want, when they are ready and will have the self confidence required to pursue their dreams.

We are not only building a future for ourselves but we are setting an example for our children. We make an effort to teach our children how money works.

My seven year old daughter now invoices us for cleaning services and some extra chores around the house on her own letterhead. Sometimes we hang on to the invoice for a few weeks just so that she has to remind us to pay. Just like in real life.

The one final thing I'll leave you with is this: If you are not where you want to be financially then do something about your current situation. Quit talking about it or blaming others – take control. Whatever you do, don't give up.

Look at what is really important to you and figure out why you want to make a change. Find that reason that will motivate, drive you and keep you going through the tough times.

Everyone has a reason - what's yours?

To your future, Dean Udsen
www.21stCenturyLifestyle.ca

PS. In my current business I'm frequently asked if I were to start over in Real Estate, where would I begin. The first call I would make is to Paul M. Hecht.

Paul taught me not only how to look at Real Estate from different angles, but helped me improve my personal productivity and confidence. As one of Paul's investment partners, we turned a $1,000 investment into almost $4 Million Dollars in Real Estate in 3 years!

I am now able to look at any business opportunity with confidence and the knowledge to properly analyze it. This knowledge and confidence has been the catalyst to ensure my family's future is secure.

Inquire About Paul's DVD Home Training,
Live Seminars & Mentoring at:

www.PAULMHECHT.com

Everyday Real Estate Millionaires™

Inquire About Paul's DVD Home Training,
Live Seminars & Mentoring at:

www.PAULMHECHT.com

Inquire About Paul's DVD Home Training,
Live Seminars & Mentoring at:

www.PAULMHECHT.com

STORY FOUR – PART ONE

PAUL

THE RISE AND FALL

"Success is the ability to go from one failure to another with no loss of enthusiasm."

~ Sir Winston Churchill

www.PAULMHECHT.com

The phone call came at 8:53am on Saturday December 4th, 1988. At the age of seventeen I was forever changed – I had just lost my mom to cancer.

At the early age of forty five, my mother was gone. She would not see me graduate. She would never attend my wedding nor have the privilege of being a grandmother. I had always pictured her sitting on the porch with my dad, the two of them growing old together. She wouldn't be doing that either. All I could think was – why?

Weren't we supposed to live to 70, 80, 90 or even 100 years and enjoy a long fulfilling retirement after age 65? If she had only lived to 45, then what was everyone working towards? It was unfortunate that only after losing my mother to cancer, did I really start to question what life was about and what really, truly mattered.

As you can imagine, that event had a significant impact on my life. I could have let her death beat me down. I could have felt sorry for myself. There was a lot of sympathy being offered and people willing to listen and give me attention.

I chose to let her death have a different impact upon my life. The only way I can describe what I took from her passing is summed up in a quote taken from Shakespeare. He said, "Life is not a dress rehearsal." I was determined to live life to the fullest.

I challenged almost every concept that society deemed customary. I challenged the traditional belief that you went to school, got good grades and then hopefully attended university. You would then obtain a well paying secure job, work until you were 65 and then retire on a company pension or with the assistance of the government.

My mother only lived until the age of forty five. That was twenty years short of retirement. She didn't even begin to enjoy the freedom that retirement was supposed to offer. That work model did not sit well with me.

Over the next year, as I entered college and began learning a little more about life, many things became apparent. If the average life expectancy in North America was approximately seventy six years of age, it meant that we would be children for 24% of our lives. We were then supposed to spend the next 47 years or 62% of our lives working. That left only 14% or 11 years enjoying our efforts in retirement. What happened if we didn't make it to retirement or when we got there we were broke? I did not like the odds.

I found that many people did not enjoy their jobs either, yet they lived and breathed them for most of their lives. How fulfilling was that? Was it worth it to work for 47 years to enjoy only 11?

How did people retire earlier so they had more time to enjoy life? Why did some people retire at 35 while others continued to work beyond age 65 because they did not have the financial means to stop working?

If there were people who had money and people who did not, then how did I become one of those people who had money?

How did I get myself into the position where I could decide if and more importantly when I wanted to retire? I didn't want to have to work until I was 65 just to realize I had only 11 years left, if I even made it that far. I was determined to find out how to get into a financial position to retire when I wanted, not when society expected me to.

That led me on my journey to find financial freedom. In my mind, financial freedom would provide choice. If I had money, then I would be able to choose if and when I worked and what interests I would pursue. I would choose when and for how long my holidays would last or where I would live. Essentially, I wanted to be able to choose how I spent my time. That was my pursuit.

And so began my quest. I was in my late teens and had a thirst for knowledge. As I had come from a middle class family, money and wealth were not subjects taught at home or at school. So I learned on my own. I began exploring the topics of finance, wealth, success and personal growth.

I came across many self-help courses. I found information on personal empowerment and wealth creation. I found several tape series that taught me how to create and design my life to suit myself and not society. I spent what seemed like a fortune at the time, but I can honestly say that my investment in myself was one of the best investments I have ever made.

Not only did I learn about the habits and success principals of some very accomplished people, but many of those concepts shaped the way that I think today. What I call my daily attitude and success habits were actually formed during those years of study.

I also examined how these people created their wealth. I discovered how they made money, what they invested in and how their money seemed to grow regardless of the economy.

The first thing I unveiled was that most wealthy people were self employed, had their own business and used a corporate entity. As a result, they paid a great deal less tax than an employee. I also found that it was quite easy for anyone to have their own corporation – it was not limited to the wealthy.

As far as investments were concerned, there seemed to be a mix of different types including but not limited to stocks, bonds, businesses, collections and real estate.

Of the people that I studied, it seemed that regardless of whether they collected art or antiques or whether they held stock A or bond B, almost all owned real estate. Not only did they have real estate in their portfolio, in almost every case, real estate held the largest percentage of their total investments. That got my attention.

Stocks and bonds seemed elusive to me and collections appeared to be a bit more specialized and speculative, but real estate piqued my interest. In my mind, investing in real estate was a real possibility.

Needless to say, at that point in my life I wasn't quite sure how to begin. I had just graduated from college, had $136.00 in my bank account, huge student loans and no real job prospects. How was I ever going to buy real estate?

It seemed that I needed to take care of some pressing issues first – like work. I decided to move up north on the promise of a well paying job to live in the cold. That way I could make enough money to cover my expenses and get started on my real estate empire.

I ended up landing a job working long hours and eating dust as a drywall taper. Not the dream job, but at least I was self employed, a partner in a drywall company and one step closer.

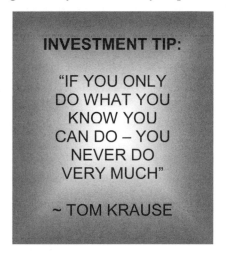

INVESTMENT TIP:

"IF YOU ONLY DO WHAT YOU KNOW YOU CAN DO – YOU NEVER DO VERY MUCH"

~ TOM KRAUSE

I would have never guessed that being a drywall taper would lead me to my first investment opportunity.

One day, as I was drywall taping a house in a new subdivision, I overheard one of our customers speaking with the electrician. The electrician was explaining to our customer that he had been trying for years to find a building lot on which to build a home. He was complaining that the new subdivision that the city was about to release to the public was hardly enough to keep up with the demand. I wasn't sure what he meant, but I was intrigued. I decided to get a little closer to make sure I overheard everything correctly.

I found out that the small city that I lived in, allowed the development of one new subdivision per year from their lands. It would then release the land in a lottery format. Buyers would put their name on a list and if their name was picked from a hat, they selected a building lot of their choice. Out of curiosity, I wanted to know what the demand really was for those building lots.

After I got home from work, I phoned the city and asked how many people were on the list and how many lots were being released.

It turned out that only 40 lots were being released with 120 people already on the buyer's list. The auction was still one week away. The demand was significantly higher than the supply. Odds were good that prices would go up.

I decided that I wanted one of those lots. I didn't want it to build on. I figured that if I could get one through the lottery system, I already had 80 potential buyers who would still want a lot. Chances were in my favor to flip the lot for a higher price if my name was pulled from the hat.

I phoned the city back to inquire about the buying process. What happened when someone's name was chosen? Apparently, the lots were to be paid for in cash within thirty days of winning the draw.

With building lots ranging in price from $25,000.00 to $35,000.00 each, I had my first challenge. I really didn't have any money saved, nor did I have any available credit. I was 21 years old and self employed. I considered my options and knew what I had to do. Like any self respecting twenty one year old, I phoned my dad.

During our conversation, I told him exactly what I wanted to do and how much money I required. I also told him that I would do all the work and split the profits with him 50/50. His response was not in my favor. In fact he suggested that I go back to school, get a real job and get a hair cut while I was at it. Needless to say, I started doubting my strategy.

After reassessing the situation, I realized that the supply and demand equation was in fact, a reality. Therefore I had decided to find another way. I wondered who would have the money and the insight to see the simple law of supply and demand in action. In my mind, it wouldn't be an employee. It would have to be an entrepreneur or business owner. It would be someone who was willing to step out and take a chance.

> **INVESTMENT TIP:**
>
> REAL ESTATE IS BASED ON SUPPLY AND DEMAND. LOOK IN YOUR OWN AREA TO SEE WHAT TYPE OF PROPERTY IS MOST LIKELY TO BE IN DEMAND IN THE FUTURE.

I realized that I needed a cash partner and decided to approach business owners to fill the role. I spoke to eleven different business owners one by one, and told them about my plan. I explained that if we were successful in obtaining a lot, I would do all the work to sell it as well as pay for any marketing costs. I also intended to negotiate a selling price that was acceptable to both of us.

All eleven business owners had similar advice to that of my father. Most gave me the impression that I was a naive twenty-one year old with just another hair-brained scheme. Listening to rejection after rejection was extremely difficult. Perhaps my dad had been right after all.

One night as I was on my way home from work, I drove by the new subdivision and decided to make one last attempt to find a money partner. I drove into a local car dealership and asked to speak to the owner. The receptionist told me that she didn't know who the owner was but that the manager could help me. Then she asked if I had an appointment.

At that point I had no other choice than to lie and ask for forgiveness later. The manager came out and we both came to the conclusion that I must have had an appointment with their competitor and that I had made the mistake.

He immediately invited me into his office and asked how he could help me. (I'm sure he thought that he was going to sell me a car that day.) I was pleasantly surprised by his attitude. It was a nice change from the manner in which I was treated by the previous business owners. I proceeded to tell him that if he could help me, I would help him. That intrigued him.

I told him all about the lottery and what I had envisioned. I then asked if he was interested in putting in the cash if I did all the work and paid for the marketing costs. We would split the profits 50/50. He said he was impressed with my thinking, liked the idea and would call me back in a few days. Wow! I finally

www.PAULMHECHT.com

had someone who listened to me and would even consider the idea. What a mistake it would have been if I had quit. I just might have my first investor!

I got back in my car with a big smile on my face and a renewed since of possibility. Then I realized that I couldn't wait a few days as the auction was only two day away.

I went back to the dealership the next day on my lunch break and told the sales manager that I needed an answer that day otherwise I would have to find someone else. Once again, he invited me into his office. We must have been on good terms, or so I thought.

He sat me down and explained to me that he loved my idea so much that he put his name on the list that morning and was going to do it himself. Just as I thought things were turning around.

I immediately realized the big mistake I had made. I gave away my idea for free. I couldn't believe what he had done. He had betrayed our partnership and we had just started.

I was just about to storm out of his office when something told me not to give up so easily. Realizing the situation, I made him another offer. I suggested that

I put my name on the list too and if mine was chosen instead of his, that he could still go 50/50 with me.

He though about it and said, "Why not, please have a seat." He then laid out his terms as follows. I was to market the property for sale and incur the cost of advertising. If we didn't have an offer in 3 months, then the property was automatically his and I would receive nothing. If we had an offer before that time, we would split any profits after all selling costs, excluding my marketing costs.

I agreed, but before I left, I requested that our agreement be made in writing. He told me not to worry about it. I told him I would write something up and that we would both sign it so that there were no misunderstandings. He agreed and we signed it the following day.

I had realized that I had just learned two very important lessons. The first was to put agreements in writing. The second was to not give up when I hit a roadblock. There was always another way.

At that point I had a potential investment partner. Maybe not the most trustworthy, but he had something I needed and at that point I had our agreement in writing. I also realized that I had nothing to lose. I was renting a

~ 141 ~

house and owned nothing. My risk was the cost of advertising. My potential profit was well worth the risk.

The day of the lottery arrived. My name was pulled and my partner's name was not. Fate? Maybe, but I wasn't complaining. I picked the best lot and my partner paid the $28,000.00. Both of our names went on the title. Having both our names on title was my protection against him trying to change our agreement again.

With the building lot in our possession, I put an ad in the newspaper and a "For Sale" sign on the property. As the city had already put in the roads and services, people could get started building homes right away. The phone calls came pouring in and we prepared ourselves to entertain our first offer.

Within ten days we had received several offers and accepted a cash offer for $40,000.00 with no conditions, closing in thirty days.

After closing costs, I had turned my $350.00 in marketing costs into a profit of $5,250.00, using other people's money. I invested my time and did not have to qualify for a loan or use my credit.

After my initial success, I decided to ask my landlord if he would sell his four-plex to me. (At the time, I was renting one of the units.) He told me that he would sell it for the right price. I asked him what he wanted for it and he said $110,000.00.

INVESTMENT TIP:

BY INVESTING YOUR PROFITS INSTEAD OF SPENDING THEM, YOUR WEALTH WILL COMPOUND AT A MUCH QUICKER RATE.

I then informed him that I would give him full asking price, with a $5,250.00 down payment, if he provided seller financing in the form of a first mortgage.

In essence, I would make my monthly mortgage payments to him instead of a bank. He would have no responsibility for the maintenance or upkeep of the property or tenants. The property would be in my name and I would have all the ownership responsibilities of a rental four-plex.

He agreed and I started to sweat. The property was in rough condition and could end up being a money pit. I decided I needed an inspection to see how bad it really was.

The inspector confirmed my suspicions. He told me how bad it was and that everything could fall apart at any minute, as well as everything that could go wrong in the future, but not to worry.

I proceeded to have my lawyer draw up an offer that included provisions for the owner to be responsible for the property if it had any serious maintenance or structural problems over the next two years. He did not sign. I did not blame him. I was too scared at the time to change the contract and decided not to proceed with the purchase since I did not have any money for repairs or maintenance. Going ahead with the deal would have put me in a risky position.

Even though I did not purchase that property, I learned another lesson. I learned that I could have bought a rental property without qualifying at the bank or having a credit check, all with less than 5% down. Once again, I learned that it was possible to buy real estate without having a large down payment, using my credit and without qualifying. All I needed to do was ask.

Shortly after that, I decided that it was time to take my dad's advice and go back to school. After four years, I graduated from University with two things – a Bachelor of Applied Arts and a new girlfriend. (Little did I know that she would one day become my wife.) So as budding designers, we moved to a new city to put our education to use.

With my schooling complete and my entrance into the corporate world underway, I decided that it was time to get back into the real estate market. We were living in a major city and noticed that real estate prices there were significantly lower than those of other major cities in the country. I knew that our thriving city would soon follow suit and that if we wanted to get into the market, we had to buy soon.

My girlfriend and I decided to purchase a house together. We worked with a real estate agent who understood what we looking for. We told him that we had $8,000.00 for a down payment, needed to take over someone's existing mortgage and the house had to have a rental suite. Seller financing would also be helpful. That was not an easy request.

It took about four months before we finally found it. It was a two bedroom house in an excellent neighborhood. It had a one bedroom suite in the basement that we could rent out to help pay the mortgage. While the property was not very appealing from the street, we knew that a paint job could remedy the situation.

The house had an existing mortgage that we could assume. We needed to come up with $38,000.00 for the down payment. To come up with the $38,000.00 we did a few things. We used my $8,000.00 savings, $1,500.00 from our joint savings and a $500.00 cash advance from our credit card to make up $10,000.00 in cash.

We then asked the seller to carry a second mortgage for us for the difference. Luckily he was motivated. He was going through a divorce and wanted to be rid of the property. He agreed to carry a second mortgage for two years and then we would have to come up with the money to pay him off. We owed him $28,000.00 and made monthly payments to him for two years.

Since my wife and I didn't need much, we decided that we would live in the basement suite and rent out the main floor of the house. We realized that we could generate more rental income from the main floor than from the basement.

We took possession of that house on Halloween. At that point, we didn't even have a bed to our names. We slept on blankets on the floor in the basement for about three weeks and then broke down and bought a bed on our credit card. But that was it, no more major purchases and certainly not on credit.

By December 1st, we still did not have a renter. The rental market was slow at the time. Since our salaries reflected our work experience and since we were paying the entire cost of the house ourselves, we were running out of money quickly.

We sat down and figured out that if we did not have a renter by January 1st, we would have to sell the house or walk away from it and everything I had saved for our down payment.

Since our efforts weren't working, we hired a property management company to advertise the house for rent. The advertising costs would come out of the tenant's first month's rent. The management company found someone almost immediately and our first tenants moved in just two days from us having to sell the house. We could breathe again.

Originally we had planned on living in the basement suite for four years (to pay down the mortgage) and then move to the main floor. After only eighteen months, my girlfriend and I both had new jobs, increased salaries and our tenants had moved on.

We moved upstairs into the two-bedroom main floor suite and we rented the basement to another very great tenant. The move upstairs felt like we had just moved into a grand palace. It was very rewarding.

Our two years were almost up and it was time to repay our second mortgage back to the original seller. We refinanced the house and paid out the first and second mortgages. Just before we refinanced, we painted the inside and outside of the home to increase the value so that the appraisal would reflect a higher value.

INVESTMENT TIP:

A GOOD QUALITY INTERIOR AND EXTERIOR PAINT JOB IN CURRENT COLORS IS ONE OF THE EASIEST AND MOST COST EFFECTIVE WAYS TO INCREASE THE VALUE OF A PROPERTY.

Several neighbors even came over while we were painting and thanked us for making the much needed improvement.

After another year in the house (a total of three years owning the home), we decided to sell. We made a profit of $40,000.00. That was more money than we had ever seen in our lives.

The purpose of us selling that house was two fold. We got married and paid cash for our wedding and honeymoon to the Caribbean. That way we were not burdened with debt payments from a wedding loan. Equally important, we still had enough for a down payment for our next house.

The next house we bought did not have a rental suite. We bought that house and lived in it for twelve months. We then had a job offer in another city and we decided to take it.

We renovated the bathroom, painted the kitchen cabinets, tiled the kitchen floor and painted both the interior and exterior of our house. We did most of the work ourselves and then sold it for a small profit of $6,000.00.

With the move to a new city, came another house purchase. We bought a freehold townhouse in a trendy neighborhood. Once again it was one of the lowest priced homes in the neighborhood. We used the money that we had made from the sale of our first two homes to pay for the down payment.

Life in a new city brought some changes. My wife became pregnant and we were expecting our first child. It didn't take long for all those beliefs I held about financial freedom and living life by my own terms to come flooding back. I now had a family to consider and I knew just the life I wanted to create for them.

While my wife and I continued to work as designers and advanced in the industry, our salaries had only marginally increased. With a baby on the way, I realized that if I wanted to get ahead financially in my field I would have to open my own service firm, rent space, hire employees and make margins on the hours that I could bill from my employees. I would also have to take on all the risk.

Instead I decided to switch to a different business model. I wanted my employees to pay me, pay my bills and build my company. That seemed significantly more lucrative. I knew just the model. It was real estate. My tenants would be my employees and they would pay me to provide them with a place to live. They would pay the financing debt, the property taxes and increase the value of my business.

Once again it was time to get educated. I obtained as much information as I could about real estate investment. I read books, listened to tapes, took several courses and paid a lot of money for my education. Was it worth it? Absolutely. While some courses did not have much value, I knew that if I learned just one thing in each course, that one idea could either generate thousands of dollars above what I paid for the course or save me thousands by keeping me from making costly mistakes.

I considered my education an investment. I understood that knowledge was priceless. I also knew that while education was a great starting point, by really immersing myself in real estate investment, I would learn so much more. No more dabbling – it was time to get serious.

While I was eager to quit my job to pursue real estate full time, I did not have the financial means to do so. Instead, I continued to work all day as a designer and spent my evenings and weekends focused on real estate.

I decided to purchase a rental property. For me, it was the most logical step to make. From everything I had read and learned, it seemed that purchasing a rental property would be the easiest and safest way for me to invest in real estate, without requiring too much experience or time. It was simple, based on facts and over time the tenants would pay off the mortgage.

I began searching for a rental property with up to four units. It had to be no longer than an hour drive from my home for ease of management. I looked for properties where the rent would at least cover the costs and I also looked for properties with a positive cash flow.

Eventually I found a property that I considered suitable. It was a triplex located approximately an hour away by car. I purchased my first investment rental property for $80,000.00 with a very small $3,000.00 down payment through some creative financing and assistance from the seller.

INVESTMENT TIP:

MANAGING THREE UNITS IN ONE BUILDING IS EASIER THAN MANAGING THREE SINGLE FAMILY HOMES.

On paper, the rental cash flow on this property looked good, but the management was tough. The property was located in a low income neighborhood with high crime. I had a property manager which helped. However, I still had to make decisions on maintenance issues and on what to do with the tenants who defaulted on rent. (The stories I heard about why people failed to pay their rent never ceased to amaze me. Maybe one day I'll write a book of all the great excuses. It would be very entertaining.)

The property was also not in very good condition, so the maintenance costs were much higher than anticipated. Since we had just purchased our town home prior to purchasing the triplex, I was extremely low on cash. I needed to find a way to create some extra money as rental properties weren't the quickest method. With rentals I had to wait for either the mortgage to be paid down or the value to increase enough to either refinance or sell.

Since I needed money fast, I thought a fixer upper would be a good strategy to generate some quick cash. Little did I know I was about to make a mistake that would almost wipe me out financially.

I decided to buy a foreclosure in Buffalo, NY, for $10,000.00 on my line of credit. I thought I had just won the lottery since I had recently paid $215,000.00 for our 900 sq ft town home just three hours away.

The foreclosure property was a 4 bedroom, 2 story home with over 2,400 sq feet. It had a driveway with a garage in the back and was located in a low income, high crime area. It was a big old house and needed lots of work. I located it through a real estate agent who helped me determine the value after renovations so that I could evaluate if I was going to make a profit.

My agent determined that after renovations, a reasonable sale price would range between $42,000.00 and $50,000.00 depending on the quality of renovations. Since my renovations were going to be exceptional, I used $50,000.00 as the price that I would receive for budgeting purposes.

Since I lived three hours from this property, I hired a contractor (using more credit) to renovate the house. He provided me with an estimated cost of $18,000.00 for the renovations and anticipated that they be complete in 60 days. In reality, they took 120 days to complete.

Not only did I not factor in any contingency amounts for any unforeseen renovations costs or overruns, I assumed that my contractor's view on quality would be similar to my own. I was wrong.

I also did not budget enough for monthly carrying costs like property taxes, finance payments, utilities and insurance while the property was vacant. If I had thought about that for one minute, I would have realized that I would only be able to carry the house for forty-five days.

As I was running out of credit, I had my agent put the property on the market before it was completely finished. As it turned out, when buyers walked into the property they did not want to see grout all over the bathroom floor, half painted walls, or listen to contractors cursing and swearing and making a mess in their "home-to-be."

On top of it, most people could not visualize what it would look like when it would be finished. Needless to say, I did not receive any offers or my expected price.

INVESTMENT TIP:

BUYING YOUR OWN HOME IS QUITE OFTEN BASED ON EMOTION. BUYING AN INVESTMENT PROPERTY IS PRIMARILY BASED ON THE NUMBERS.

The agent and I also listed the property a little higher than the current market value since my renovation costs had escalated. Buyer's did not care if my costs were higher, if I had overruns, paid too much, took too long or had unexpected events. Buyers saw my house along with comparable houses. Mine was priced higher than the others and therefore not very popular.

After a few months of marketing the property for sale normally, I had the agent market it as a lease-to-own.

That didn't work either. Anyone who was interested couldn't come up with the small down payment I required, even though I was willing to provide financing for them.

After three expired listings, three price reductions and eighteen months, I decided to rent the property just to cover my costs. I then found out that the rent I could obtain for the property was about $500.00 per month less than my holding costs. Therefore, I would lose $6,000.00 per year if I rented it. The property was not increasing $6,000.00 per year in value to offset the costs.

Then I decided to try and sell it myself. Not because the agent wasn't a qualified agent, but because I thought outside the box.

The national average price was more than three times the price I was asking. Therefore I though I would give the property national exposure. I put it on eBay®.

I offered the property as a low down, no qualifying investment property at $35,000.00. I offered the buyer financing if they put down $3,000.00. The financing I offered was just enough to cover my own financing costs. The buyer would take over my other carrying costs such as property tax, insurance, heat and utilities.

It worked. I found someone on the west coast who did not take the financing I was offering. Instead they paid cash of $32,000.00 and wanted it for an investment property. My tiresome ordeal was over.

Between renovation overages and two years of holding costs, I had officially lost over $30,000.00 on a property that cost only $10,000.00 to buy initially.

Since my holding costs on this property were over $1,100.00 per month, I had to come up with this money every month in addition to contributing to a household. I tried to pay this with my job income for two years but my salary did not cover the additional payments. The extra payments often went onto a line of credit and credit cards.

When the property was sold, I finally had some relief. However, even after the sales proceeds; I still had almost $15,000.00 in credit card debt. With my salary it would have taken approximately two more years to pay this debt off. I did not want to wait that long just to pay off the debt.

With the success of the eBay® sale, I decided to try another strategy and thus my eBay® real estate business began. Since the market in Buffalo was slow at the time, I could put offers on properties with my real estate agent that would have a very long possession date and I could ask for a long timeframe to waive my conditions. This gave me time to find another buyer.

INVESTMENT TIP:

SOMETIMES YOU HAVE TO MARKET A PROPERTY TO A DIFFERENT TYPE OF BUYER THAN INITIALLY THOUGHT IN ORDER TO SELL IT.

I found investment properties that would generate positive cash flow. With prices so much lower than the national average and good rents, many properties had a healthy cash flow. This made them attractive as investment income properties.

My plan was to put the property under contract and then sell that contract to another investor. That investor would close on the original offer I had with the seller. In essence, they were buying my interest in the contract that I had negotiated. This was called an assignment of contract.

I successfully sold several contracts and was beginning to develop a good business. I had many investors request that I set up contracts for them before I put the properties on eBay® so that they could avoid the auction competition. If an investor purchased a property from me previously on eBay, we would agree on what they would pay me for my service and what they were looking for. I would then arrange it.

I sold contracts for anywhere from $2,000.00 to $7,500.00 depending on the terms of the contract, the size of the property and the competition for my contract. The largest property contract I assigned was for a twenty-three suite apartment building.

At one point I was selling three to four contracts per month at an average of $3,000.00 per contract while working my full time day job. I had no direct costs as the buyer assumed all the costs of the transaction. Within the first few months, I had paid off all the debt I had accumulated from the renovation project loss in Buffalo.

I had found another way to make money in real estate without going to the bank, qualifying or having my credit pulled. I was also now building a business.

After time, a few other people caught on to what I was doing and started doing the same thing on eBay®. Many of my competitors would find run down properties in extremely bad locations and sell them to other investors at a lower price than the properties I was marketing. They were lower in price for a reason. This gave all of us a very bad reputation.

INVESTMENT TIP:

PROPERTY MANAGERS ARE GREAT SOURCES OF LEADS FOR POTENTIAL BUYERS.

With more and more people offering contracts and quality getting worse, I decided it was time to shut down my online real estate business.

It was also around this time that I sold my triplex to my property manager for a small profit. He owned several properties at the time and could not qualify for more mortgages from his bank. He gave me a $20,000.00 down payment and I provided financing for him. I had a small monthly cash flow from the financing payments and relieved myself of the property management.

I then started looking for other real estate opportunities. My wife and I decided to move to the other side of the country to an area where real estate values were still affordable and the economic outlook looked very promising for growth. It was there that I joined an

~ 160 ~

existing real estate business. I sold all my real estate and invested in the company. It was a service company and I had three other partners. Although the product was excellent, for many internal reasons the business struggled. While the four of us tried to grow the business, I took home very little pay. Most of the profit was reinvested into the company.

INVESTMENT TIP:

WHEN YOU HAVE MORE THAN TWO PARTNERS IN A PARTNERSHIP, YOU GIVE UP SOME CONTROL IN THE DECISIONS THAT ARE MADE.

Also, during this time, my wife and I had our second child. We decided that since it made no financial sense to have her work and pay for someone else to raise our children, she would stay home with the kids. With her not working and with me not making enough money to pay the bills, we started living off our lines of credit and credit cards again. We did this with the hopes that the business would turn around and eventually turn a sizable profit.

We lived like this for two years before I finally left the partnership. The debt however still remained. We were maxed out to the tune of over $100,000.00 in personal debt, not including our mortgage. The monthly payments were enormous.

For almost another year, I tried to pay off the debt myself by taking extra labor jobs that I could do in the evenings and on weekends.

At that point, our goal each month was to pay the minimum payment on each credit card. However the minimums kept growing as the debt accumulated. Eventually creditors were calling us at home, we couldn't sleep at night and we were arguing constantly. We had reached the end of our rope.

We decided we needed professional help from a bankruptcy trustee. He gave us some ideas and advice. On his advice, I made a proposal to our creditors and offered them a payout amount with a manageable payment plan. In order to receive an accepted proposal, I needed 67.0% of our creditors to vote in favour of my proposal. I received 66.7%. Since I did not get the 67.0% minimum requirement, I was automatically forced into bankruptcy. I was officially bankrupt. What a horrible feeling.

I was trying to get to financial freedom and yet I ended up bankrupt. I felt like I had failed at everything and nothing was working. I had lost myself and my self worth as I had tied my personal value to my bank account.

We did not tell anyone about the bankruptcy for almost two years. We lived with the shame and no one knew our secret. I do not wish that on anyone. It was a terrible place to be.

In the darkness, we did find some light in knowing that the credit card game was over. We no longer had to struggle every month just to try and make the minimum payments. We had a chance to start fresh. I was determined not to ruin our second chance.

After all the mistakes I had made and everything I had learned with our real estate transactions, my wife and I agreed that we had made the most money in real estate over any job we ever had.

However, at that point, my wife desperately wanted me to get a secure job so that we could get back on our feet. I knew that not only would a regular nine to five job not provide the financial freedom I was seeking; it would kill my dream and my spirit.

I knew in my heart that real estate was the answer and fought her on getting a regular job. If I was going to continue to pursue real estate investment as my job and go beyond my wife's wish, I knew that if I screwed up again I would lose her. I had to consider that very carefully.

After many serious discussions together, we came to the conclusion that we both wanted each other to be happy and that life was too short to have regrets. We knew that as long as we had each other, our family and our health, we would be okay.

That's when we decided to go for it. My wife hesitantly agreed, but stepped up and supported our venture all the way. I made a promise to myself that we would have financial freedom and that we would not go back to a life of financial poverty.

Two years after declaring bankruptcy, we were millionaires. Yes, millionaires. I made good on the promise to myself and my wife and we often reflect on our situation. We often wonder how it all happened so quickly.

Some days I still have to pinch myself. I always knew in the back of my mind that I would be a millionaire one day. I truly believed it in my soul and knew it was just a matter of time.

When I was in my early 20's, I set the goal to be a millionaire by the time I was 30 years old. At age 30 I was far from a millionaire and a few years later I was bankrupt.

So how does someone go from being bankrupt to having a million dollar net worth in just two years? Please let me share this part of my story with you - it is my favorite.

Inquire About Paul's DVD Home Training,
Live Seminars & Mentoring at:

www.PAULMHECHT.com

Inquire About Paul's DVD Home Training,
Live Seminars & Mentoring at:

www.PAULMHECHT.com

STORY FOUR – PART TWO

PAUL

THE COMEBACK

"It's not whether you get knocked down.
It's whether you get back up again."

~ Vince Lombardi

www.PAULMHECHT.com

After my bankruptcy, I reset my goal to be a millionaire by the age of 35. That was only two years. I didn't know exactly how I was going to do it. The fact that our credit was destroyed and we had no cash or ability to qualify for loans made the task a little more challenging. Once again, I had to dig deep and get creative.

INVESTMENT TIP:

A MILLIONAIRE IS WHEN THE DIFFERENCE OF ALL ONE'S ASSETS MINUS ALL ONE'S LIABILITIES IS $1M OR GREATER.

As one of my friends once told me, "when you are lying on your back, all you can see are the stars." That was true. I was already at the financial bottom, I could only go up.

The one thing I did know was that the vehicle to my million dollar goal would be real estate. I also realized that I had to take massive action to achieve it.

I focused on my goal to be a millionaire in twenty four months. Not only did I focus on it, I imagined in my mind what it would feel like. To the point where I actually imagined going into the bank and depositing several checks for $100,000.00 and $200,000.00 dollars each and looking at my net worth statement showing a one million dollar net worth. The feeling was amazing. My reality was less so.

The one thing that I realized was that I couldn't just dream about it, I had to focus and commit to doing it. I had to get straight to work to achieve this goal in such a short period of time.

My plan was to put as much energy and effort into the real estate market as I possibly could. I wanted to plant as many real estate seeds as possible - seeds that would grow into large money trees. I was willing to work day and night for twenty four months if I had to. I was determined to get out of our situation as quickly as I could and never have that financial stress again.

Here's what I did.

I partnered up with a business associate who was also a real estate investor. He had invested all his own money into real estate and had run out of his own capital. In a practical way, it was ridiculous. We both had no money. However, the one thing we both had was the desire and determination to shoot for the stars. We both managed to scrape together $500.00 each to invest into our real estate business.

~ 169 ~

We started a rent-to-own business with real estate. We used a combination of methods to acquire properties. The first was to approach landlords who would let us rent their properties and also give us an option to purchase the property within a specified time. That was usually two to three years. We were also allowed to sub-lease the property and therefore we would sub-lease the property to someone else and we would give them an option to buy the property at a higher price than we were able to buy it at.

INVESTMENT TIP:

CONTRARY TO POPULAR BELIEF, IT DOES NOT TAKE MONEY TO MAKE MONEY IN REAL ESTATE.

If our tenants exercised their option, then we would exercise our option at the same time and take the spread between the two contracts. We had spreads of between $20,000.00 and $50,000.00 per contract. It would depend on how good of a deal we negotiated with our landlord and the value we could offer to the sub-tenant.

The second method of acquisition was to have investors buy the properties and we would manage the tenants, the contracts, the marketing, the maintenance and everything associated with the management of the property.

We had it set up so that once the property was sold, our investors would make the equivalent of 19.0% annual return on their investment. Their money was secured by real estate as they were on the property's title. They were passive investors who did not want the typical hassle of tenants, yet they understood the security and benefits of investment real estate.

We would make about the same as the investor. Overall our cash profits ranged from $15,000 to $30,000 per deal with this method. The upside was that if the tenants did not exercise their option with us, we could always exercise our option with our investors.

As it turned out, several of the tenants did not exercise but we still did. At the time we exercised our option, we were buying the properties under market value. Some we sold immediately, while others we held onto and rented out.

Our other strategy was to acquire properties from the pre-foreclosure market. People had missed their mortgage payments for several months and the banks were about to foreclose and take their house. At that point, we could still negotiate with the owner. Once the bank had foreclosed we would have had to deal with the bank directly. We chose to deal with the owners.

What we noticed was that several homeowners would get behind on payments for a variety of reasons such as illness, death in the family, job loss or injury on the job. Once they got one or two months behind, the mortgage lender's lawyer would issue a demand letter along with the lawyer's bill. People often couldn't catch up, nor could they pay the legal bill. Therefore they would lose their home.

We would screen people to see if this was a pattern or a "one time" occurrence. We would then often purchase the home by taking over the existing financing. We usually bought the home at a discount since the loan was often lower than the total home value.

With some owners, we would pay off the arrears and then let them rent the property so they would not have the additional costs of a move. Sometimes we even gave them an option to buy the home back in the future.

We were very upfront that we were giving them a second chance however in the event they missed any rent payments, they would be evicted immediately. They also had to understand that as tenants, they were under a tenancy agreement and were no longer the owners.

Of the ones we gave an option to, approximately 60% bought the homes back. The other 40% did not and we ended up with properties at a discounted price. With this business model we acquired twelve properties in twenty-four months.

Some people simply wanted to sell their property. We either bought the property and immediately resold with seller financing on it, or we sold our contract to another investor. Either way we flipped another nine properties.

INVESTMENT TIP:

BEING FLEXIBLE AND ADAPTABLE IN YOUR STRATEGY WILL ALLOW YOU TO MAKE MONEY IN A MARKET WHERE OTHERS CAN'T.

We also bought several rental properties with other investors. Again, we would manage the tenants and any renovations. The investor would supply the financing and the cash. We would split any net profits 50/50. Our projects always had a minimum return of 30% ROI annually to the investor. They were happy and so were we.

In fact, we just closed the sale of a rental property that we had purchased 18 months ago with one of our investors. The investor called me to personally thank me for providing them with a successful project resulting in their profit for almost $100,000.00 in 18 months. We received the same amount. They had invested a total of $110,000.00. That equals a 90.9% return on their money. Annualized, it's 60.6%. That's a great feeling.

These particular investors re-invested with us and we purchased a four-plex together. We found a run down building with poor property management. Then we completed a significant renovation including new kitchens, new bathrooms, new flooring, paint, new exterior stucco, new roof, new boiler and new garage doors with automatic openers.

The building was in an area where rents were average. We took an average rental building and transformed it into a very nice property. We increased our rent role by approximately 60%.

My partner and I started out with a $1,000.00 ($500.00 each) investment. In twenty four months we had turned our $1,000.00 investment into over $1.2 Million dollars in equity and cash profits from our lease options, sandwich lease options, flips and rentals. Our rate of return on our money was phenomenal. Our desire and effort had proven to be more powerful than our lack of money.

During the time right after my bankruptcy, I had also put my efforts into another real estate venture. I had another associate who was also a real estate investor. He was starting to grow his portfolio of properties and was in the process of selling his single family and duplex rental properties so that he could buy an apartment building.

He approached me about being part of the venture. As I had just declared bankruptcy, I didn't have the money to get into that size of project.

However we talked for a while and he had taken on a new business partner. They had the capital to run the project but they wanted someone on site with construction and design background to help with renovations.

He proposed that I be part of the renovation team and help with the design and sub-trades. He suggested that he and I physically complete most of the renovation work so that we could control costs and see what it actually took to renovate an eleven unit apartment building. Plus, we paid ourselves what we would have paid someone else to do the work. That cash helped pay bills at home.

Neither one of us had taken on such a large renovation project before. I knew it would be hard work physically. On the other hand, I wanted to learn what it took from being on the inside of the apartment building business.

INVESTMENT TIP:

MEETING OTHER INVESTORS AND SHARING KNOWLEDGE AND SKILLS MAY LEAD YOU TO YOUR NEXT OPPORTUNITY.

Even though I had no money, I knew that wealth was in the ownership and equity of real estate. I told him I wanted to be paid in part in equity in the building. Since we were all motivated by the same goal, to increase the value of the building - everyone agreed.

We figured out a formula by which I put a value on my time. I then took that amount and was paid half the amount in cash and took the other half as an equity interest in the building.

My wife desperately wanted me to take it all as cash so that we would be more financially stable at home. I made sure that we had enough money to put food on the table. I knew the only way to get back on my feet quickly was through ownership.

At home, we made sacrifices and lived a very lean existence. With all the physical work and the lean times at home, I lost more than ten pounds. Many people would enjoy the weight loss; however it was too much for me.

I was working during the day renovating an apartment building and then working many evenings and most weekends on my other rent-to-own business. As tiring as it was, the sacrifice paid off.

That partnership acquired two more apartment buildings of which I owned shares. For those two buildings, I did not do any physical labor. I invested some money and continued to provide design consultation on those projects. I put in the effort up front and continued to grow my investment. In total this partnership owned 38 units.

During the six month period of renovating the first apartment building, my rent-to-own partnership provided cash profits from our flips. That helped out with living expenses at home.

When all was said and done and when my twenty four month deadline was up, I sat down on my thirty-fifth birthday and found myself with just over a million dollar net worth.

I went from being bankrupt to achieving my goal of becoming a millionaire. It was a lot of work in a short period of time. It was also a lot of money.

Was it easy? Absolutely not.

Was it worth all the hard work? Absolutely.

It was a lot of effort, action and sacrifices on me and my family. Part of the reason that it was not easy was that I did not make it easy on myself. I gave myself two years and did whatever it legally took to achieve it.

In retrospect I could have slowed down, taken more time and had a more balanced life. Some say that I got lucky. I'd have to agree. I was lucky enough to put in the effort required to be in the right place at the right time and then know what to do when an opportunity presented itself.

Although many people I knew were working overtime at their 9-5 jobs, often in the evening and on weekends just like I was, I did not want to spend the rest of my life sacrificing that much time away from my family.

My family and I made a lot of sacrifices and we went through some very trying times. I know that during the time of our financial hardships, the stress was often too much for my wife to bear. Our marriage suffered for many years.

We would often joke that even if my wife wanted to leave, she couldn't because she didn't have any money to go. We have since mended our relationship and as a result, it is stronger than ever. Not in spite of those trying times, but because of them.

All I can say is that I am so grateful for my wife's support and willingness to stay by my side and pursue the dream. She is a great friend and an incredible mother to our two beautiful, healthy children.

While I have worked very hard to be where I am today, I realize that I am extremely fortunate. If I sold everything that I own today, invested the money, lived off the interest and maintained my existing lifestyle, I would never have to work another day in my life. But how much fun would that be?

So today, I continue to invest in real estate and other related ventures. I also enjoy assisting others realize their real estate investment goals in a variety of ways. Whether it's through speaking engagements, live training, mentoring or acting as their agent, I am thrilled to be able to help others turn their real estate dreams into reality.

Thank you for taking the time to read my story as well as the three stories before mine. My hope is that they educate and inspire you to take at least one step forward on your own path to financial freedom.

The journey is worth it.

Sincerely,

Paul M. Hecht

Author | Speaker | Investment Coach | Real Estate Agent

Inquire About Paul's DVD Home Training,
Live Seminars & Mentoring at:

www.PAULMHECHT.com

Everyday Real Estate Millionaires™

Inquire About Paul's DVD Home Training,
Live Seminars & Mentoring at:

www.PAULMHECHT.com

~ 181 ~

GETTING STARTED

Free Wealth Reports
& E-Newsletter

Receive your complimentary EVERYDAY *Real Estate* MILLIONAIRES™ E-Newsletter, Audios and three complimentary Wealth Building Reports including:

Wealth Report #1 - How To Make $1Million And Retire With Only 2 Houses, Regardless of the Market

Wealth Report # 2 - How To Consistently Earn 8% to 14% Inside your RRSP, IRA or 401K

Wealth Report #3 - The 7 Mistakes that Beginner Investors Make that the Gurus Don't Tell People

EVERYDAY *Real Estate* MILLIONAIRES™ E-Newsletter shows how regular people make money with real estate and avoid common mistakes by learning proven strategies for any market. Filled with practical and useful information, you'll realize that you do not need to own 100 homes, dedicate your entire life to investing or even be a landlord to become an EVERYDAY *Real Estate* MILLIONAIRE™. Get these Free Wealth Building Reports at…

Get the Free Wealth Reports and E-Newsletter at:
www.PAULMHECHT.com

CONTINUING EDUCATION

StarterKit

The StarterKit includes over 20 different real estate strategies highlighting the advantages and disadvantages of each one. It helps you…

IDENTIFY your unique skills, resources and personality so that you can select strategies that are best suited to you.

GAIN FINANCIAL CONTROL & CLARITY by understanding your personal investment criteria.

UNDERSTAND THAT YOU DON'T HAVE TO BE A LANDLORD or deal with tenants to make money in real estate.

THAT A LACK OF MONEY, financing, retirement, divorce or bankruptcy cannot stop you. Use the StarterKit to help you succeed.

UNDERSTAND WHY PEOPLE FAIL and how you can increase your chances for success.

Get the StarterKit at:

www.PAULMHECHT.com

CONTINUING EDUCATION

Live or DVD Home Training

LIVE TRAINING

Attend our Live Training and receive the most up-to-date current market

DVD HOME TRAINING

forecast, network with other like minded people, personally ask me any question you like and do it all in an interactive and creative, hands-on, focused environment.

Watch the Live Training which has been professional recorded onto DVD so that you can learn in the comfort of your own home, when it's convenient for you. Watch it as many times as you like without any travel expenses.

"Everyday people can do this. It's down to earth, Paul's approachable and his wealth formula is clearly articulated."
- **Darryl Kelly, Investor**

Inquire about our Live and DVD Home Training at:

www.PAULMHECHT.com

EITHER WAY, YOU'LL DISCOVER:

- Why people who want to be rich never will be until they do this 1 simple thing
- Natural market cycles and signals to watch for
- How to invest when you are self employed, unemployed or retired
- How to buy without cash, credit checks, loan applications or verification of income
- How to turn a negative cash flow property into a positive one and eliminate petty phone calls from tenants forever with Lease Options
- How to flip property without renovations
- How to assign/sell contracts to other investors
- The fastest way to build wealth with real estate
- How to optimize Joint Ventures and Investors
- How to invest other people's money and do it safely
- Why investors will give you money to invest even if you have none of your own
- How to interview mentors and how to tell a fake
- Property Analysis Software & Legal Agreements Paul Uses

"I will never invest the same way that I did before. This gave me the confidence and the WHOLE picture of what real estate investment is all about. Thanks for the REAL Training!" - **Christine Maloney, Self Employed**

Inquire about our Live and DVD Home Training at:

www.PAULMHECHT.com

CONTINUING EDUCATION

Real Estate Mentoring

 The majority of our mentoring students have taken part in other real estate seminars and training, yet found something missing. Our hands-on mentoring program fills in those gaps and...

ACCELERATES your path to wealth

BREAKS THE BARRIERS AND GUIDES YOU through the in's and out's of real estate

PROVIDES A PRESONALIZED ACTION PLAN based on an assessment of your resources, skills, time, personality, interests, goals and financial statement

ALLOWS YOU TO ASK questions and receive an experienced second opinion about your current and future investing

HOLDS YOU Accountable

Get Mentored by Paul at:
www.PAULMHECHT.com

More Everyday Successes

"Paul was one of the first people who got me educated on real estate investment. I knew a little bit about it before but Paul gave me the tools to go out and put it into action.

I applied what I learned and became a millionaire with Paul's strategies. I've known Paul for about eight years now and I owe it all to him."

Carrie Hutten, Mortgage Intelligence

"Thought maybe we could offer a testimonial for you or you could use us as another example of everyday people that have made millions in real estate (we made a few – thanks to you).

Tammy and I were both blue collar workers in the courier business when we got started. We now own $10 million worth of real estate.

I finally quit my job last year as I was too busy with real estate. Let us know if we can do anything for you. Thanks" **Roger Panchuk, RTA Venture**

Get Mentored by Paul at:

www.PAULMHECHT.com

"I had been investing in smaller residential rental properties for about two years and was still very much getting my feet wet in real estate investing.

I was immediately drawn to Paul's style. I am not a big fan of high pressure sales tactics; quite the opposite. Paul had a genuine interest in helping me.

With Paul's help, I purchased over a dozen rental units within a few years using joint venture strategies."

Marc Tews, CGA

"True success in real estate comes about with a long term outlook and a focus on relationships, systems, and follow through. Not to mention what you can create in your life when you have a big enough WIIY and when you are truly clear about what you want.

Paul helped us identify our ideal investment properties, which we still hold today. I definitely recommend Paul's training to my close friends and business associates." **Darryl & Eva Kelly, Landlord**

Get Mentored by Paul at:
www.PAULMHECHT.com

"We always knew that smart real estate investing can be one of the most successful ways to generate wealth. We turned to Paul Hecht six years ago. Not only did Paul mentor and guide us through the often confusing and intimidating world of real estate investing; thanks to Paul our real estate portfolio is healthy and growing and we are well on our way to the financial freedom a regular pay check could never give us."

Tim and Joleen Fluet, Pharmacist & International Real Estate Investors

"Paul M. Hecht was a major catalyst for me to take that leap and really take control of my life by investing in real estate.

I had read all the books and taken many seminars before but nothing beats real life experience and Paul definitely had the street experience and the knowledge it takes to be successful. I was immediately able to go out, use Paul's strategies and increase my portfolio within just a few months. I would highly recommend Paul to anyone getting started in real estate or like myself wanting to take your investing to the next level."

Warren Hansen, Investor & REMAX Realtor®

Get Mentored by Paul at:
www.PAULMHECHT.com

"In one afternoon we learned more about investment real estate than we had learned over the past two years of reading books and attending other seminars.

We've attended other real estate seminars before but the other speakers seamed like they we holding back, and just giving tidbits of information. Paul was honest and laid it all out for us, explained everything and was very welcoming when we had any questions. We purchased our first investment property and we owe a lot of that to Paul." **Dave Mulder, Architectural Technologist**

"Paul has given me advice on real estate matters that have significantly increased the value of my real estate holdings. He knows real estate.

Since working with Paul I have noticed that he uses his considerable experience to look at broad market trends in the industry which helps him identify specific opportunities in regional markets. He is always learning and assimilating new information which helps with his ability to pick up trends well ahead of the crowds.

Bottom line is Paul Hecht is a nice guy who makes you money!" **Dr. Lance J. Couture, Optometrist**

Get Mentored by Paul at:
www.PAULMHECHT.com

Everyday Real Estate Millionaires™

We need your success story here....

HOST AN EVENT, SEMINAR OR LECTURE

Speaking

Bring Paul into your organization or your next event. Paul inspires and encourages individuals and audiences alike. He proves that the average person starting out against the odds can be successful and lead an abundant life by creating opportunities and thinking outside the box.

Paul is able to present a variety of real estate and success topics including what it takes to be successful and achieve results in both business and in life.

Not only is Paul's story an example of what is possible, he has the incredible gift of transforming often complex strategies into easy to understand concepts for the average person to grasp.

To book a speaking engagement, please email

MEDIA@PAULMHECHT.com

www.PAULMHECHT.com

www.PAULMHECHT.com

MEDIA PROFESSIONALS

Interviews

Paul is regularly interviewed on Radio & TV across North America and hosted THE REAL ESTATE INVESTMENT & SUCCESS SHOW featuring everyday people who had achieved significant wealth & success.

"Paul is a 'fundamentals' based investor who knows his stuff!" - Doug Blackwell, 1510AM KFNN Financial News Radio

"Paul's advice is so simple and makes so much sense, everyone should take notes!" - Anita Finley, Boomertimes Magazine & Radio

"Absolutely fantastic interview, perfect!" Monica Puig, 880 AM Latin Biz Talk Radio

"Great guest with fabulous information." Wendy Robbins, KTOS 101.9FM Radio

To request a Media Kit or Interview, please email

MEDIA@PAULMHECHT.com

~ 195 ~

www.PAULMHECHT.com

FINAL THOUGHT

Inspirational Quote

Many people believe that in order to be successful they have to have all the answers, their situation in life has to be perfect, and all the lights have to be green before they get started.

This often stems from a fear of failure. I have failed many times in life and in business. The fact is that successful people fail ten times more than the average person simply because the average person never tries. Power is in taking the first step, not knowing what lies in the second. However, without taking the first, the second step never appears.

This passage was written by mountaineer, W.H. Murray during his Scottish Himalayan Expedition in 1951. I hope you enjoy it.

> "…but when I said that nothing had been done
> I erred in one important matter.
> We had definitely committed ourselves and
> were halfway out of our ruts.

We had put down our passage money –
booked a sailing to Bombay.
This may sound too simple, but is great in consequence.
Until one is committed, there is hesitancy,
the chance to draw back,
always ineffectiveness.
Concerning all acts of initiative (and creation),
There is one elementary truth
the ignorance of which kills countless ideas
and splendid plan:
that the moment one definitely commits oneself,
then providence moves too.
A whole stream of events issues from the decision,
raising in one's favor
all manner of unforeseen incidents,
meetings and material assistance,
which no man could have dreamt would have
come his way.
I learned a deep respect for one of Goethe's couplets:

*"Whatever you can do
or dream you can,
begin it.
Boldness has genius,
power and magic in it!"*

www.PAULMHECHT.com

Everyday Real Estate Millionaires™

Visit

www.PAULMHECHT.com
TODAY
Get Started On
Your Path To Financial Freedom NOW!

~ 199 ~

www.PAULMHECHT.com

Visit

www.PAULMHECHT.com

TODAY

Get Started On
Your Path To Financial Freedom NOW!

~ 200 ~